The Calm in My Storm

THE CALM
IN MY STORM

The Calm in My Storm

Chiso Ori Uko

XULON ELITE

Xulon Press Elite
2301 Lucien Way #415
Maitland, FL 32751
407.339.4217
www.xulonpress.com

© 2023 by Chiso Ori Uko

All rights reserved solely by the author. The author guarantees all contents are original and do not infringe upon the legal rights of any other person or work. No part of this book may be reproduced in any form without the permission of the author. The views expressed in this book are not necessarily those of the publisher.

Due to the changing nature of the Internet, if there are any web addresses, links, or URLs included in this manuscript, these may have been altered and may no longer be accessible. The views and opinions shared in this book belong solely to the author and do not necessarily reflect those of the publisher. The publisher, therefore, disclaims responsibility for the views or opinions expressed within the work.

Unless otherwise indicated, Scriptures marked ESV are taken from the ESV® Bible (The Holy Bible, English Standard Version®) copyright © 2001 by Crossway, a publishing ministry of Good News Publishers. ESV® Text Edition: 2011.

Scripture quotations taken from the Christian Standard Bible. (CSB). Copyright © 2017 by Holman Bible Publishers. Used by permission. All rights reserved.

Scripture quotations taken from the Holy Bible, New Living Translation (NLT). Copyright ©1996, 2004, 2007 by Tyndale House Foundation. Used by permission of Tyndale House Publishers, Inc.

Scripture quotations taken from the New King James Version (NKJV). Copyright © 1982 by Thomas Nelson, Inc. Used by permission. All rights reserved.

Scripture taken from The Passion Translation (TPT). Copyright © 2017 by Passion & Fire Ministries, Inc. Used by permission. All rights reserved. thePassionTranslation.com

Scripture quotations taken from The Message (MSG). Copyright © 1993, 1994, 1995, 1996, 2000, 2001, 2002. Used by permission of NavPress Publishing Group. Used by permission. All rights reserved.

Scripture quotations taken from the Amplified Bible (AMP). Copyright © 2015 by The Lockman Foundation. Used by permission. All rights reserved.

Scripture quotations taken from the Contemporary English Version (CEV). Copyright © 1995 American Bible Society. Used by permission. All rights reserved.

Scripture quotations taken from the Holy Bible, New International Version (NIV). Copyright © 1973, 1978, 1984, 2011 by Biblica, Inc.™. Used by permission. All rights reserved.

Scriptures marked AMPC are taken from The Amplified Bible Classic, containing the amplified Old Testament and the amplified New Testament, 1987. The Lockman Foundation: La Habra, CA.

Paperback ISBN-13: 978-1-66287-970-8
Ebook ISBN-13: 978-1-66287-971-5

Praise for 'The Calm in My Storm'

"This book chronicles Chiso's heartbreaking and tumultuous marriage experience. As a parent, it is difficult to see your child go through a painful ordeal, but I am incredibly proud of her for having the courage to share her story with the world. My "Ada Ada" as I fondly call her has written a powerful and compelling memoir that provides a window into the reality of an abusive marriage. Her writing is raw and honest, and she doesn't hold back in describing the emotional and psychological abuse that she endured.

Chiso's unwavering spirit, love for Christ and determination to overcome her circumstances is an inspiration to us all. Her book is a testament to the strength of the human spirit and the resilience that comes from knowing that Jesus our Redeemer lives forever."

– Lady Nnenna Uko.

"Anyone who has experienced the tragedy of infidelity knows that words cannot capture the heartbreak and sense of loss one feels. However, in this work, Chiso graciously captures not only the emotional devastation so common to such experiences but the faithful and merciful guidance of the Lord through a journey of spiritual awakening and soul restoration. This book is both a manual of do's and don'ts for the inexperienced, as well as a source of solace for the wounded heart. Well worth the read."

– Pastor Natacha Byrams.

"The Calm in My Storm unveils the precursors of sexual vices and the addictive nature of sexual perversion. The book systematically highlights red flags and time-tested secrets that will set anyone free from the satanic hold of sexual immorality.

I am most intrigued by the way the author uncovers the subtle, deceptive nature of premarital sex, adultery, spousal abuse, and how she exposes her most vulnerable moments. This book is a must read for all youth, parents, ministers, and counselors involved in ministry - whether with young adults, couples, or students."

– Assumpta Onyinye Ude, Ph.D.

"A needed powerful book in a time when the art of enduring is lost. You can literally sense the presence of God so heavy while reading. This book both encouraged and challenged me. I am certain it will change lives for Jesus."

– Dr. Adeola Oluwatimilehin.

"Chiso Uko's *The Calm in My Storm* is a painfully candid yet beautiful look into agony and the tumultuous way we all have to journey through it. The light at the end of the tunnel is clear from the title, but the journey to liberty and joy is still turbulent despite the undertones of hope. Whether you are in the grips of a painful divorce or battling an entirely different harrowing issue, this book is for you.

– Mrs. Ife Oyeleye, host of *'Already in You'* podcast.

"Chiso's extraordinary story inspires courage, hope, and faith in the steadfast love of God even in the midst of unimaginable heartbreak and trial. This book is such a gift."

– Mrs. Nkem Chukwu.

THE CALM IN MY STORM

*Following the Spirit through
Adultery, Manipulation, Abuse, and Divorce*
Chiso Ori Uko

*The three things essential to writing a book after
surviving a bad marriage are
Unction from the Holy Spirit,
Words from the Holy Spirit, and
the desire to tell your story as He leads.*

Dedication

*To the Holy Spirit,
My Help and my Shield, my best Friend and the One Who stood with me in the fire and carried me through it unscathed.*

I dedicate this victory to You. ♥

Table of Contents

Foreword xv

Introduction – God is My Provider xvii

Chapter 1 – Watch and Pray 1

Chapter 2 – The Spiritual Component 13

Chapter 3 – The Calm in My Storm 25

Chapter 4 – My Nightmare 37

Chapter 5 – The Psalms 53

Chapter 6 – The Dream 67

Chapter 7 – The Lord is My Helper 85

Chapter 8 – The Daniel Fast 101

Chapter 9 – God's Permissible Will 115

A Final Word about THE Man in My Life 125

Epilogue – The Lord is Always With You 127

About the Author 135

Foreword

"A broken and contrite heart, O God, You will not despise." (Psalm 51:17 ESV)

In over 33 years of ministry in the local Church, I have walked with many people that were unable to recover from the "storms of life". Though many may have started out strong in the Lord, the circumstances of life have caused them to shrink back and stop pursuing God's calling on their lives. To find someone who has been through the fire, and yet testifies of God's goodness in the midst of it, only magnifies the power of God to redeem, to sustain, and to heal a heart that's been broken.

I first saw Chiso Uko in a Worship Service. I noticed her because of her worship. Her face radiated the glory of God. It was as though a light was shining down over her, as she poured out her worship to her Father. She quickly became an active part of our Church, and then a part of our family, and now my daughter in the Lord. I watched as she stepped into the lives of those around her when they needed it most, and ministered Jesus to them. She has a special way of making everyone around her feel as though they are family. I would have never known all that she had walked through until I read her story.

I was asked to make edits on an original manuscript. My heart broke as I felt the depth of hurt and betrayal that Chiso had lived through. I could not put it down and finished reading it in one sitting. She wrote with such honesty and transparency.

It was as though I had picked up something holy, and I felt as though I could not touch it. God was greatly glorified in the writing of this. Herein lies the power of the testimony. Revelation 12:11 speaks of overcoming the enemy by the blood of the Lamb, and by the word of our testimony. Chiso's story is proof that God is a Great Redeemer, and that He is able to bring beauty from the ashes of our lives. After reading her story, I remember saying to Chiso that I was reminded of the three men in the fiery furnace, where it was said of them that not only had the fire not harmed them, but there was not even the smell of smoke on them (Daniel 3:27). Similarly, I would never have known that Chiso had been through such an intense fire, or inferno, because there was no evidence of destruction, or even the smell of smoke, on her life. Only the glory of God remains. Be encouraged as you read this, that this same God walks with you, with the power to redeem, to sustain, and to heal.

-Rev. Mary Jane Murphy,
Calvary Chapel International Worship Center.

Introduction

God is My Provider

> "Chiso, you have what you need to do what the Lord wants. God has provided what you need to do what He wants."
> – **Ife Oyeleye** *'Already in You'* **podcast**

As a little girl, I made a vow to the Lord that no matter what everyone around me was doing, I was going to save my virginity until my wedding day.

I had lasted some twenty-six years.

He said he was a virgin too, but now I will never know.

Just like that, all the vows I had made to the Lord about not letting go of my virginity until after my wedding went out the window. All for that momentary pleasure of experiencing the "high."

> "For what will it profit a man if he gains the whole world, and loses his own soul?" (Mark 8:36 NKJV)

I want you to understand that as we cultivated the habit of living in sin, we also got used to the thrill of the illegal. You know that excitement and the high you get when you do something you know you should not? Yes, that high. We got addicted to it. Sin is addictive. You lie once, you want to lie again. You steal once, you want to steal again. The fact that you "get away with it" makes you want to daringly do it again. You see, the person in a relationship says to themselves, "I know that fornicating is wrong, but very soon this man or this woman will be my spouse and it will be okay". The problem is that, when you do get married, the sex is no longer illegal. By default, it no longer has the excitement that doing something you should not do has. So, what do you do? You look for the next best thing that can give you that high, that thrill, the next illegal thing to do. Fill in the blank.

For some, it is nonsexual, like drugs, alcohol, or other addictions.

For others it is pornography, masturbation.

For others, it is adultery.

> "I have avoided sharing my story for long enough.
> It is time to be obedient to His voice,
> lest He begin to scream at me."
> - Chiso

Chapter 1

Watch and Pray

It must have been sometime around 2 a.m. on July 6, 2016, when the call came through. I was in a deep sleep, but the consistent ringing of the telephone woke me up. I picked up the call; it was from one of my best friends. With a pensive tone, she said "Chiso, you need to pray; watch and pray." It was a strange call. A few seconds later, the call was over. I went back to sleep, only to be woken up a few minutes later by another phone call from my husband; his was with an even stranger tone. I do not remember what he said, but I remember it was odd. He seemed to be "checking in", or fishing for information on what I had heard.

My husband and I met in college in the Spring of 2008. Amongst other things, we found common ground in the fact that we are both Nigerians. A few months later, on Mother's Day 2008, after more than a few dates, we made our relationship official. Our relationship lasted 8 months.

While we were together, in this first bout of our relationship, we would go to church together occasionally, read devotionals together, etc. All the while erroneously consoling ourselves with the fact that while we fondled with a lot of heavy petting, we did not actually have sex. Hence, we were 'okay' in God's eyes. However, our relationship was not one that honored God. How could it? Our hearts had never met this Jesus. We knew of Him, but neither of us had ever come face-to-face with Him.

Towards the end of that year, the passion I had for him waned. As it was my custom, I went back to Nigeria for the Christmas festivities. And, while I was there, my heart pulled further away from him. On my return to the US, in January 2009, I ended the relationship.

At the time, we had both been attending weekly Bible studies at a campus ministry we both agreed to be a part of. But we were inconsistent. We were one leg in, one leg out.

About the time I ended the relationship, we'd been invited to the campus ministry's out-of-state annual national conference. Valentine's Day was on the horizon; therefore, he tried persuading me to mend the relationship. In my bid to escape his skillful badgering, I jumped at the opportunity of attending the conference when I was invited again. It was going to be a peaceful weekend, I reasoned. He also decided to come along with the hopes of convincing me to change my mind about our relationship. Little did we both know what - excuse me, Who - was waiting to meet us there. On the first night of the conference, he responded to the altar call and gave his life to Jesus. The next day, February 7, 2009, I came face-to-face with Jesus, and I surrendered my life to Him. It was an encounter that forever rocked my world, and the rest, as they say, is history.

After the conference, when we returned to our campus, we remained friends; good friends at that. We were now both consistent members of the ministry and saw each other very frequently. At some point, we began studying the Scriptures together. One night, a couple of friends from the ministry were staying over with me at my parents' house and he was one of them. We read through the book of Job together, with all pure intentions, until we got a little too close for comfort.

While nothing physical happened, our souls were getting too riled up for God's liking. So, we each got an individual stern talking to from the Lord. I do not know what the Lord said to him, but the Lord said to me in no uncertain terms, "I need you both to walk with Me separately; the two of you are not joined together".

Season of Turmoil

Nine years later, when the season of turmoil started in 2016, I often thought back to that night and that admonition from the Lord. Did God mean we were not to be joined together for the time being? Or ever? The latter would have made my life a whole lot easier and would have spared me all the tears and heartache that ensued in marriage.

But I digress.

After the Lord's admonition, we stopped reading the Bible together. We remained friends but kept a healthy distance. He transferred to another university - Howard University - while I remained at the University of Maryland Baltimore County; the distance was healthy. We would run into each other at church – we attended the same church - sometimes at Bible study meetings, and at other ministry events. At least we were not seeing each other daily.

Fast forward a year later to 2010. At the time, there was what I would call "the marriage talks" at our church. We were encouraged to seek the Lord about our future spouse. I was not particularly interested at the time. However, in the spirit of being obedient, I prayed for my future spouse as directed. I would pray vague prayers like, "Lord, wherever he is, keep him safe, let him know You." The truth be told, I was only twenty-two and was not really yearning for marriage. I only prayed about it because, as young people, we were encouraged to do so.

If I could go back, I would advise my younger self to pay more attention to this instruction.

I have heard it said that the two most important decisions in life are:

1. The decision to accept Jesus Christ as Lord and Savior and
2. The decision of whom you marry.

While the first has eternal consequences, the second impacts your life on this earth. Consequently, it is a key player in deciding where one spends eternity.

Whilst praying for my future spouse, every now and then, I would see his image flash before my eyes. I dismissed it as, "I am just not over him yet." Sometimes when I would see him in person, depending on how he wore his pants, I would catch a glimpse of his boxers which would instigate a thought that'd usher in many other impure thoughts reminding me of our past. Then, I would immediately admonish my mind to focus on purity and on Jesus and forget the past. I shared these occurrences with one of my mentors and she prayed over my mind. After that, the thoughts ceased, and I continued to half-heartedly pray for my future spouse.

He and I were both a part of the worship team at church. One Saturday, during worship practice, he stood up to converse with the Worship leader. I initially had my head down, looking at something on the floor. As soon as I lifted my head and saw him standing there, I heard God say: "This is the one. The one your heart was made for. The one you love."

I thought to myself, "Absolutely not! No way!" I willed the ground to open and swallow me. The thought of him as my husband so repulsed me that I said to the Lord, "If this is really You speaking, You are going to have to miraculously pour out Your love in my heart for this man."

On the drive home I was quiet. A friend was sleeping over at mine. When we got home, I opened my mouth to tell her what I had heard. But then I heard the Holy Spirit say, *"...But Mary treasured up all these things in her heart."* (Luke 2:19 NIV). Therefore, I kept silent. Over the course of the next couple of days, I tried to share what I had heard with my sisters, but I heard Him say it again. So again, I said nothing.

I would later find out that he had been on a 40-day fast and during the fast, the Lord told him that I was his wife. His response to God was, "God, if it is really You, You must directly speak to Chiso. You confirm it with her." Hence, God ambushed me during worship practice.

A few weeks later, we met with the Pastors of our church. After being instructed to pray for three months to confirm that God was indeed speaking to us both, we began our courtship in March 2011.

I share all this back story to say, up until that point, we had our process in good order. I read about people like Elizabeth and Zechariah.

> *"In the days of king Herod of Judea, there was a priest of Abijah's division named Zechariah. His*

> *wife was from the daughters of Aaron, and her name was Elizabeth. Both were righteous in God's sight, living without blame according to all the commands and requirements of the Lord. But they had no children because Elizabeth could not conceive, and both of them were well along in years."* (Luke 1:5-7 CSB)

When I read this, I thought to myself that they did things the right way and that they loved God. As a matter of fact, the Bible records that they were righteous in God's sight, living without blame according to all the commands and requirements of the Lord. They followed all His proper channels. Yet, they had no children.

Please, do not misunderstand me. I am not comparing myself to Zechariah nor Elizabeth, not in a million years. Rather, what I am getting at is that feeling of being entitled to our desires after we've done all things according to His defined precepts. That blame-game with God when we feel our "right-standing" with Him should shield us from all perils. I know I felt that way when I was confronted with many trials that ensued after I got married.

When everything crumbled, I stood and I pointed my finger at God. My exact words were, "God, I did not ask You for this man, I did not beg You for a husband. So, why have You brought this on me?"

The first nine months of our courtship was long distance. I was in Nigeria preparing to go to medical school in Antigua while he remained in the U.S. So, it was safe. We would talk for hours, sharing our dreams about our future. We planned it all out – the wedding, the marriage, all of it. The distance kept us safe from crossing the physical boundaries. Initially, our plan was to court for two years with me being away in the Caribbean and then return to the U.S. for about another year of courtship/wedding planning. However, *"A person's heart plans his way, but the Lord determines his steps."* (Proverbs 16:9 CSB)

I ended up not going to medical school in the Caribbean and, by January of 2012, I was back in the U.S. The first few months together in person were pure. By April of 2012 though, things changed.

Red Flag Alert

At first, it was subtle. We would watch movies alone at my place and somehow, in the dark room, our hands would find their way to each other's bodies. Next, we graduated to making out at different times, either while we watched movies or sometimes even in our cars. We mastered the art of fornicating without really having any sexual intercourse. Thereafter, we'd get on our knees to be forgiven by our Father. Little did we know that the only people we were fooling were ourselves. We kept forgetting He said, *"What should we say then? Should we continue in sin so that grace may multiply? Absolutely not! How can we who died to sin still <u>live in it</u>?"* (Romans 6:1-2 CSB).

Our culture of sin was the beginning of the end. Do not get me wrong, our God is mighty and the redemptive power of His blood through His Son is very potent against any sin-type. However, at that early phase, we had begun building a foundation in our hearts and in our future home for sin to flourish. I understand that there were other factors that contributed to our falling out of place, however, with the knowledge I have accrued through my experience, I understand the importance of walking in purity and not only in matters of relationship and marriage. We have been called to walk in purity in every aspect. Our God is holy, and He demands that we also walk in holiness, for our good and for His glory.

While physical purity is important, it does not stop there. James writes, *"But each person is tempted when he is drawn away and enticed by his own evil desire. Then after desire has conceived, it gives birth to sin, and when sin is fully grown, it gives birth to death."* (James 1:14-15 CSB).
So, it is important to guard our hearts and to guard what we allow in. Just because you are not fornicating does not mean your mind and your heart are pure before the Lord.
There is a saying in Nigeria's colloquial English language, pidgin English, "Body no be firewood." A stern acknowledgement of the frailties of our bodies.

It all started in our hearts and our minds.
The more time we spent together, the more our hearts and our bodies wanted each other. The more our hearts wanted each other, the easier it was to conceive the thought of engaging in heavy petting. So, we began to lust after each other. Every opportunity we got, we indulged.
Throughout Scripture, there is a resounding theme concerning fornication, sexual sin, and youthful lust:

> *"Run from sexual sin!"*
> (1 Corinthians 6:18A NLT)

> *"Flee sexual immorality"*

(1 Corinthians 6:18A NKJV)

"And have nothing to do with sexual immorality, lust, or greed – for you are His holy ones and let no one be able to accuse you of them in any form."
(Ephesians 5:3 TPT)

"God's will is for you to be holy, so stay away from all sexual sin. Then each of you will control his own body and live in holiness and honor - not in lustful passion like the pagans who do not know God and His ways."
(1 Thessalonians 4:3-5 NLT)

"Flee also youthful lusts…" (2 Timothy 2:22A NKJV)

"There is more to sex than mere skin on skin. Sex is as much spiritual mystery as physical fact.…"
(1 Corinthians 6:16 MSG)

The Bible says to flee, that means to run away. Run like your life depends on it!

Remember Joseph? He understood his assignment. He was alone in a house with a beautiful woman as she lusted after him. The Bible records that she, Potiphar's wife,

"She grabbed him by his garment and said, 'sleep with me!' But leaving his garment in her hand, he escaped and ran outside." (Genesis 39:12 CSB)

I ask myself: Why would a grown man run away from a woman?

Joseph had enough God-given wisdom to understand that sin brings only one thing: death.

The problem with sin is that when you get accustomed to it, it rules your members. Yes, I am aware of the times we live in; I am aware of the "expected" fornication that comes with being in romantic relationships. I get that. However, it does not change God's stance on it; that it is a sin, and it is immoral.

Throughout our courtship, we began to isolate ourselves from others in the fellowship, not intentionally, just by default. Perhaps, we were so lost in fornication, and we did not see that we were out of fellowship. This went on from 2012 up until 2015. We got married in May of 2015.

By March 7, 2015, two months prior to our wedding, we finally had sex.

Watch and Pray

Red Flag Alerts

As you journey with me through my marital trials, pause and reflect on the ▭ Red Flag Alerts I failed to recognize and heed along the way. Review this first chapter and consider how you might have done things differently if you encountered a similar situation.

> *"God's will is for you to be holy, so stay away from all sexual sin. Then each of you will control his own body and live in holiness and honor - not in lustful passion like the pagans who do not know God and His ways."* (1 Thessalonians 4:3-5 NLT)

▭ **Red Flag Alert:** At first, it was subtle. We would watch movies alone at my place and somehow, in the dark room, our hands would find their way to each other's bodies. Next, we graduated to making out at different times, either while we watched movies or sometimes even in our cars. We mastered the art of fornicating without really having any sexual intercourse. Thereafter, we'd get on our knees to be forgiven by our Father.

What would you have done in this situation?

Why should we consider this as a Red Flag Alert?

In 2 Timothy 2:22, the Bible says to flee youthful lusts, which means to run away, run like your life depends on it!

What consequences could a couple encounter by not heeding Red Flag Alerts and warnings from God?

Review the other Scriptures mentioned in this chapter where God warns of the dangers of sexual sin.

What did you learn from these verses?

Chapter 2

The Spiritual Component

I vividly remember sitting in a chair as my makeup artist prepped my face for my wedding day. When she was finished, I sat there and composed my vows to him. Cue the waterworks. I wept uncontrollably as my sister held me. They were good tears. Not like the ones I would later shed. No, these were tears of overwhelming joy. I was hours away from saying "I do" to the man of my dreams, so, I let them flow. Predictably, my makeup artist was not pleased, *sigh*.

The day was beautiful. We were surrounded by loved ones. Approximately, 500 guests came to share in our joy, both invited and uninvited. There was lots of dancing, good food, and lovely music to merry the heart. Yes, my heart was content.

It must have been about midnight when we left the ballroom and walked up to our hotel room. In the Nigerian culture, it is customary for the couple to be gleefully sprayed with money on their wedding day as they dance. It is a big deal. When we got to our hotel room, the money was there waiting for us. So, what did we do first? We counted it. Strange? I know, but wait, it gets interesting. After counting, we had dinner. Next, we took a shower together. What happened after the shower should have set off bells in my head.

▪ **Red Flag Alert:** I expected him to make advances towards me. What I remember is him telling me he was tired and wanted to sleep.

Normally on the wedding night, particularly for two people who are new to this world of sexual intimacy and have tasted it three times at most, you are hungry for it. No amount of fatigue can stand in the way of that yearning.

▪ At that point, I should have known. I should have gotten on my knees to start warring in prayer with the understanding that the foundation of our marriage may not be stable, but I did not.

The Forbidden Fruit Syndrome

What happened? Why weren't we excited about moving into marital intimacy as a couple? Does it have to do with eating the "forbidden fruit"?

My siblings and I do this all the time; if one of us has something the others do not, the rest of us would make it our mission to battle for it. When we succeed, we derive satisfaction in knowing we have captured the "forbidden fruit" - a scarce resource. What happens, though, is the minute the resource is in excess, forget it, it loses its appeal.

Take Adam and Eve for example.

> *"The Lord God took the man and placed him in the garden of Eden to work it and watch over it. And the Lord God commanded the man, "You are free to eat from any tree of the garden, but you must not eat from the tree of the knowledge of*

> *good and evil, for on the day you eat from it, you will certainly die."'* (Genesis 2:15-17 CSB)

They had one job, and the instructions were simple. You get to have everything in this garden. Anything your heart desires, you can have, but do not touch the tree with the forbidden fruit.

> *"Now the serpent was the most cunning of all the wild animals that the Lord God had made. He said to the woman, "Did God really say, 'You can't eat from any tree in the garden'?" The woman said to the serpent, "We may eat the fruit from the trees in the garden. But about the fruit of the tree in the middle of the garden, God said, 'you must not eat it or touch it, or you will die.""*
> (Genesis 3:1-3 CSB)

Fast forward to July 2015, two months after our wedding. Now, up to this point, I had never considered myself a dreamer – someone God talks to through dreams – because I could not really recall a moment when the Lord had spoken to me in a dream. However, on this night, He did. It must have been sometime around 2:00 a.m. or 3:00 a.m. I had been asleep for a while when suddenly, I dreamed that my husband was gone. I did not know where. But in the dream, he just left, and he was gone for good. It was almost like when a person goes off to the military but with the twist of having no intention of coming home ever again. In the dream, I began to sob uncontrollably. I broke out in a sweat. I was hysterical and it was near impossible to calm me down. I did not realize what was happening until my tears and the sweat and the despair woke me up.

The Calm in My Storm

When I woke up, he was in bed beside me. He tried to calm me down.

When he asked what was wrong, I said, "You were gone, you just left, and I did not know where you had gone nor why."

He responded by reassuring me that he was right there, and it was just a dream. He held me, wiped my tears, made love to me, and I forgot about the dream.

> "And the Lord said, 'Shall I hide from Abraham what I am doing'" (Genesis 18:17 NKJV)

God was persistent. He showed me the dream two more times in the next few months, but I thought nothing of it. I do not even remember rebuking and canceling it in the place of prayer. We simply went on with life as normal. *Sigh.*

> "Surely the Lord God does nothing, unless He reveals His secret to His servants the prophets." (Amos 3:7 NKJV)

Am I saying God caused this premonition and ensured it? No. Rather, I believe He allowed me to see what was coming to avert it in the place of prayer. Remember, everything is spiritual before it is physical.

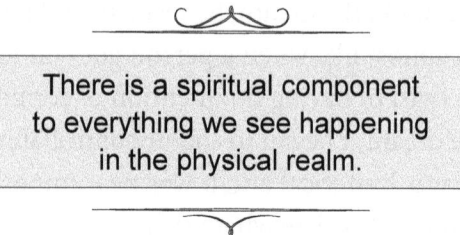

There is a spiritual component to everything we see happening in the physical realm.

> *"While we do not look at the things which are seen, but at the things which are not seen. For the things which are seen are temporary, but the things which are not seen are eternal."*
> (2 Corinthians 4:18 NKJV)

Over the next few months, it was married life as usual. We had our verbal disagreements, for sure. Some even carried over to the next day when we forgot God said, *"And 'don't sin by letting anger control you.' Don't let the sun go down while you are still angry, for anger gives a foothold to the devil."* (Ephesians 4:26-27 NLT).

Everything God does has its purpose. Every Word He speaks is for a reason, nothing is ever idle or without intent. In His instruction to not let the sun go down while we are still angry, He is lovingly letting us in on a secret. As long as we are upset and not speaking with our spouse, there is someone speaking lies to both of us – the devil.

We have a real enemy, and his job is to steal, kill, and destroy not just our lives but our marriages as well. So, unbeknownst to us, in those moments of being upset with one another, the enemy was sowing seeds of bitterness.

If I could insert one piece of advice here, it would be this: husband and wife, settle that disagreement before the sun goes down. Do not let it linger. Sit and stare at each other for hours if you must. Break the ice. No matter what you do, do not give a foothold to the devil. This applies in every relationship, not just married couples. Parents, reconcile with your children and siblings reconcile with one another. You matter too much to each other and to the kingdom of God to allow a misunderstanding to drive a wedge between you. If you attempt to settle the misunderstanding but the other party will not speak with you, then begin to pray over that person. Declare blessings and the goodness of God over them. For as long as you are blessing them, the enemy will not trick you into cursing them in your heart.

Don't Give the Enemy a Foothold

Now, back to misunderstandings. I grew up in a family of eight. Having a family that large meant misunderstandings were bound to occur. With my siblings, those arguments were never anything serious and we would invariably make up. After all, all we had was each other. Even my parents would have misunderstandings. However, my siblings and I were all wise enough to know not to interfere because before we knew it, they would make up and be best friends again. So, my perspective on arguments has always been, "Say 'yes' to the mess. Disagree, yes. Leave, no."

I have learned that there are two types of people. There are the ones who are quick to say sorry and the ones who are quick to forgive. He was the former while I was the latter. I lovingly called him the peacemaker. More often than not, he was the first to apologize while I was the first to actually let it go.

It was not until much later I realized being first to apologize did not mean his heart was cleared of the argument. I began to learn that when he said "sorry" it was only for the sake of keeping peace and not because his heart was free of whatever the issue was.

Being a type A person, every few months I would say to him, "How are we doing? Are there some things you have noticed that I can work on?"

His response was always the same, "No, there is nothing, you are perfect."

A few months later, I would ask the same question only to get the same response. So, as far as he led me to believe, all was right in our world. We went on with married life as usual.

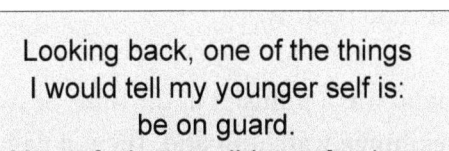

> Looking back, one of the things I would tell my younger self is: be on guard.
> Most of what we did was feed our flesh with different forms of entertainment.

We would sit in front of the television for hours on end, sometimes days, binge watching tv shows. Forgetting God's warning:

> *"Be alert and of sober mind. Your enemy the devil prowls around like a roaring lion looking for someone to devour. Resist him, standing firm in the faith, because you know that the family of believers throughout the world is undergoing the same kind of sufferings."* (1 Peter 5:8-9 NIV)

> *""I have the right to do anything," you say - but not everything is beneficial. "I have the right to do anything - but I will not be mastered by anything."* (1 Corinthians 6:12 NIV)

There is nothing wrong with television and there is nothing wrong with being entertained. Afterall, we had the right to do anything, but we forgot that not everything is beneficial. So, while we entertained ourselves and consumed things that we knew did not glorify God, we let our guard down spiritually.

Red Flag Alert: We forgot that we have an enemy whose job is to steal, kill, and destroy.

My husband was a minister at the time. So, we could spend a whole week binge watching and, then, a day or two before he was called to minister, things would get "spiritual" in our house. We would declare a fast on the day of his ministration. We would remember to pray the night before.

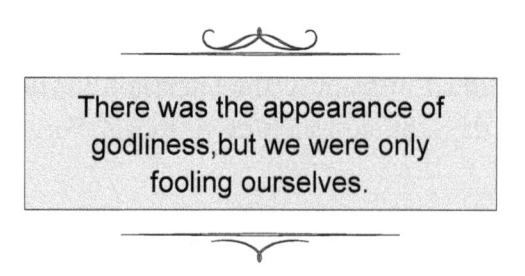

> There was the appearance of godliness, but we were only fooling ourselves.

Of course, God would always move mightily because God can and will use anyone and everything for His glory. The only problem was, the more we forgot about our enemy, the more our enemy gained ground.

He would go preach to people, then we would come home, and binge watch all sorts of TV shows or movies, none of which glorified God.

He would go declare God's holiness and His salvation to the lost. The Holy Spirit would deliver people from the kingdom of darkness, literally breaking chains, and we would come home and feed ourselves with content that made the lust of our eyes, the lust of our flesh, and the pride of our lives thrive. God warned us clearly:

> "Do not love the world or anything in the world. If anyone loves the world, love for the Father is not in them. For everything in the world - the lust of the flesh, the lust of the eyes, and the pride of life - comes not from the Father but from the world. The world and its desires pass away, but whoever does the will of God lives forever."
> (1 John 2:15-17 NIV)

Red Flag Alert: As a result of everything happening in our hearts and in our home, we also stepped away from our church community. It was not that we stopped going to church, we were present, we just were not *present*. Our love for the Lord was growing cold.

> "Let us think of ways to motivate one another to acts of love and good works. And let us not neglect our meeting together, as some people do, but encourage one another, especially now that the day of His return is drawing near."
> (Hebrews 10:24-25 NLT)

> **Please hear me and hear me loud and clear:
> Church Community Matters!**

Of course, the Lord is more than able to help you stand in Him, but there is a blessing of being in fellowship and in unity with other believers. When you surround yourself with other believers, the Bible explains that they sharpen you in your walk. They also can pinpoint areas of your life that do not look like Jesus. In so doing, we stir one another up and encourage each other to remain focused on Jesus. That is also why it is important to have prayer partners and mentors who hold you accountable.

Married life continued like this from May 2015 until April 2016. During this period, we laughed together, cried together, grew together, and also loved deeply; or so I thought.

The Spiritual Component

Red Flag Alerts

As you continue this journey with me through my marital trials, pause and reflect on the Red Flag Alerts I failed to recognize or did not heed. Review this chapter and consider how you might have done things differently if you encountered a similar situation.

Red Flag Alert: I expected my new husband to make advances, but he told me he was tired and wanted to sleep.

> *At that point, what should I have done?*

> *What happened? Why weren't we excited about moving into marital intimacy as husband and wife?*

Red Flag Alert: We forgot that we have an enemy whose job is to steal, kill, and destroy.

> *Why is the enemy out to destroy your marriage relationship?*

> *Why is it dangerous for you to ignore or forget about this powerful enemy?*

> *How are you going to fight this enemy?*

> There was the appearance of godliness, but we were only fooling ourselves.

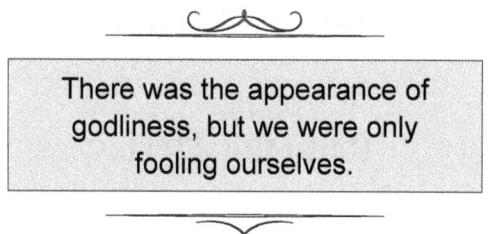

Red Flag Alert: It was not that we stopped going to church. We were present, we just were not *present*. Our love for the Lord was growing cold.

What can happen when your love for the Lord has grown cold?

What must you do to reignite that love relationship with God?

> Please hear me and hear me loud and clear: Church Community Matters!

Chapter 3

The Calm in My Storm

There it is again, the catchy phrase "the calm in my storm." What does it even mean? A quick search with Google explains it as: "the quiet period immediately before the trouble." Except mine was a tad different. Mine was the quiet period, a safe place **during** the trouble.

What do you do when all you have known and loved, what you *perceive* as the very core of your being, comes crashing down before your eyes like a sandcastle? In those moments, if you remain still long enough to hear His whisper, then go searching for it. The "it" being:

> "Then Job arose, tore his robe, and shaved his head; and he fell to the ground and worshiped. And he said: "Naked I came from my mother's womb, And naked shall I return there. The Lord gave, and the Lord has taken away; Blessed be the name of the Lord." In all this, Job did not sin nor charge God with wrong." (Job 1:20-22 NKJV)

It is poetic, but we do not always get there; at least not immediately.

I heard it in my heart again, "The Calm in My Storm."

I remember a little over ten years ago, in 2009, I had just met Jesus and as I read through books in the Bible like Job and James, I read about the blessing of trials.

After reading, I was so zealous for the Lord, I said to Him, "Lord, give me trials. I want trials."

While I cannot say I would take back my words if I could, I will say nothing could have prepared me for the storm I would be thrust into beginning in April 2016. It would not reveal itself with all its might until July 6, 2016.

In life, we tend to remember days for joyous memories. What I remember most about July 6th, is the sound of my heart beating so loudly with one thought, "There is no air left for me to breathe; I am undone."

Toward the end of March 2016, my husband and I visited Nigeria for my brother's traditional wedding. While in Nigeria, we made the decision to start trying to get pregnant. As you can imagine, we had a good trip. When it was time to leave Nigeria, I forgot my passport in my home state and did not realize it until it was too late to turn back. As a result, my husband had to return to the U.S. without me. It was no problem; it would only be for two days, and we would be together again. Little did I know that the man I hugged and said goodbye to at the airport would not be the same man I would meet upon returning to the U.S.

When I got home, he was physically present, but at the same time, distant. I tried to read him but failed at it. He was in pharmacy school at the time, and I knew it was hard on him. Therefore, I convinced myself it was just the stress of school.

Red Flag Alert: In the past, with his school, it had always felt like we were in it together. We celebrated his successes together and we cried together when an exam went poorly. It felt like a partnership. With April came change. As his absence continued, I realized something was off, but I just could not put my finger on it. He began to come home really late at night. Then came a night when I went to bed without him and woke up with the other half of our bed empty. He never made it home.

I went to his school the next morning to drop off some things and he seemed almost aloof and nervous at the same time. In my naivety, I believed school was weighing very heavy on him. One day of him not coming home turned into two days, and then into seven. Seven days turned into weeks and, before I knew it, months had gone by. Something was terribly wrong.

Finally, I asked him why he had to sleep at school, he told me a friend was helping him study and was only available at night.

Red Flag Alert: In that moment, I should have prayed, "Father, give me wisdom to see through deception. Give me discernment to recognize light from darkness." But I did not.

During this time, I wrestled with my thoughts:

"Perhaps, I should speak with someone? Perhaps not. It was not wise to let others in. The mature thing to do was to believe my husband was so inundated with schoolwork, he was studying into the late hours of the night; unable to come home?"

Then, one night, he was away "studying," I was alone in our bed and right before I drifted off to sleep, I heard the enemy say, "why don't you just take off your wedding rings? What is the point?"

What? I was stunned into silence.

I said, "God forbid," and dismissed his comment, but I did not forget it.

I had mentioned to my best friend that something was wrong, and I told her what the enemy said. But we did not realize what the enemy was planning. However, what I realized was that my marriage was under attack.

Red Flag Alert: During those months, I began to hear the gentle whisper of the Holy Spirit say, "I am your Help and your Shield"

"My shield?" I wondered, "What exactly do I need a shield for?"

Over and over, He kept saying the same thing to me. I was perplexed. In all honesty, I tried to ignore it, but His sheep distinctly hear His voice. On the rare occasions I would see my husband, I said to him once or twice, "we need to talk with someone, something is wrong." I suggested we speak with one of the Pastors over us.

His response was, "we do not need anyone in our business."

Red Flag Alert: As the days and weeks went by, I hardly ever saw my husband. After some time, I noticed some of his clothes and shoes were missing from the closet. Then, I realized he was waiting for me to leave the house to come home to get some things.

One day I was ill, so I stayed home from work. Sometime around midday, my husband walked into the house to collect some of his clothes and was startled to find me at home. I explained to him I was sick. I will never forget how unmoved he was when he learned of his wife's illness. My words fell on deaf ears. He took his things and left.

Our one-year wedding anniversary came around in May 2016. Though it was a national holiday, my husband never came home. I think he called at some point in the day and said he had schoolwork to do.

I cried.

He came by the next day and had this urgency to try to sleep with me. However, try as hard as he might, he could not successfully make love to me. It had never happened before.

Red Flag Alert: So many bells went off in my head. First off, we had not slept together in perhaps two months, so why now the sudden urgency to do so? Secondly, why could he not complete it? I kept all this to myself.

On Father's Day, we went over to his parents' house to celebrate with his family. Before we left our house, we had an argument about him not being home. Again, I told him we needed to speak with a Pastor to counsel us. Of course, he refused.

At his parents' house, we watched a movie about Hosea. For the strangest reason, I remember looking at the person portraying Hosea and seeing myself in the character. I did not know what it meant. My husband and I had only ever been with each other, neither of us were promiscuous. I could not wrap my mind around what I was sensing in my spirit. I kept it all to myself.

Now, I love flying. I always have. I think more so since I have gotten to know Jesus. I especially love when I fly by myself because for some odd reason, it is always such an intimate time with Him. Something about being so high up in the air makes me marvel at and appreciate God's creation and it quiets my heart enough to hear Him. During this season, my work flew me out for a conference the week of June 22. While on the plane, as it was customary, I began to write to the Lord. Something peculiar happened. Although I was writing to the Lord, it was almost as though God began to write through me to my husband. Through Him, I saw myself write, "I forgive you."

I was so confused.

Next, the Lord began to write through me this long letter of forgiveness to my husband. I had no idea what was going on, but it seemed the Lord was trying to communicate forgiveness over something very specific my husband had done. When my flight landed, I sent it to my husband. I do not recall his response, but I do remember my text to him led to an argument.

My family loved my husband and had accepted him as a son and a brother, not just as an in-law. When they would call and ask after him, I would always make excuses as to why he was not home. Other times, I would intentionally call them when I was on my way to work so when asked, I could tell them my husband was either at home or at school. This went on for months.

I was lonely and my heart hurt. It was the worst kind of hurt because I had no idea what was going on. I also could not talk with anyone because I was still "protecting my husband and our marriage."

The July 4 weekend came with all the revelation.

> *"For all that is secret will eventually be brought into the open, and everything that is concealed will be brought to light and made known to all."*
> (Luke 8:17 NLT)

Sometime in the preceding week, a classmate of my husband's went to some church friends of ours and told them they had heard some things about my husband and another girl. Of course, I had no idea and they said nothing to me. I tried to reach my husband on July 4. As usual, he gave me an excuse as to why, although it was a national holiday, he had to be in school.

Two of my best friends, who had also heard about my husband and the girl, called me and when they asked how I was doing, I broke down crying. They immediately came over to my house and I told them my husband had been gone for months. They still said nothing to me of what they had heard. They comforted me and eventually went home.

A few days later was when the two strange calls woke me up at 2:00 a.m. on July 6, 2016.

I was at work when I got the third call. I was standing on the stairwell leading to the fourth-floor at my office. Two of my best friends and my friend's husband were on the call. First, they asked me where I was, next they asked if we could meet up to talk in person. I knew something was wrong and I did not want the suspense of waiting until after work, so I asked them to tell me. I began to shake vehemently. I couldn't stop. They went on to tell me they had heard some things about my husband. The previous night when they called me at 2:00 a.m., they had found my husband in a bedroom in a strange house with another woman.

My husband was with another woman?

I went numb. I did not understand what they were saying.

My husband is having an affair?

Immediately after their call, I sent a text to my Pastor and one of my best friends who was in the U.K. at the time: "I just heard some things about my husband. If they are true, I will divorce him." I wrote.

My Pastor's response was, "Noooo, Chiso. The Lord will help you!"

My friend said nothing. She simply got down on her knees and began to pray.

I turned to Google and searched: "How to get a divorce in the State of Maryland." Suddenly, it was as though someone turned my Google search into a foreign language. I could not, for the life of me, understand anything on the screen. In frustration, I closed the web browser, tried calming my racing heart, and processed what they said.

My husband was having an affair?

While I did not understand the magnitude of what I had just walked into, I had a sense I had just been thrust into a fierce spiritual battle.

My husband must have figured out our mutual friends had called me because he called me frantically, panicking. I asked him what he had been doing in the girl's house.

His response was, "I was helping her with a school assignment."

I think my heart tried to protect me from the shock. While I was hearing what sounded like my husband was sleeping with another woman, I found myself getting angry at my husband for being in a girl's room late at night. In some way, my brain rationalized it all – he was studying and, therefore, his offense was his inappropriate choice to study in another woman's room. He should have known better.

The rest of the afternoon was a blur. My mind remained focused on replaying the fact my husband, the man I married, was having an affair.

My husband agreed to meet me at home so we could talk. When he came home, I asked him if it was true. He looked me in the eyes and denied it. He then told me he hardly even knew the girl. He insisted he was only helping her with a school assignment. He swore to me, "on the name of the Lord", it was all a lie. I shudder now even as I remember his words. After we spoke, he left.

The next morning as I lay alone in our bed pondering divorce, I heard God say, "I have not released you from this marriage."

"God," I said. "I told him I would love him, but if he crossed the line and committed adultery, I would be done with him.

God replied, "That is called *conditional* love which is not **My** type of love. Stay and fight for your marriage."

I knew I had to obey God's mandate.

———✻———

The Calm in My Storm

Red Flag Alerts

As you continue this journey with me through my marital trials, pause and reflect on the Red Flag Alerts I failed to recognize or did not heed. Review this chapter and consider how you might have done things differently if you encountered a similar situation.

Red Flag Alert: I realized something was off, but I just could not put my finger on it. He began to come home really late at night. Then came a night when I went to bed without him and woke up with the other half of our bed empty.

I was blind to the reality of my husband's behavior. What should I have done instead of denying the obvious?

Red Flag Alert: In that moment, I should have prayed, "Father, give me wisdom to see through deception. Give me discernment to recognize light from darkness."

Instead, I wrestled with my thoughts:
"Perhaps, I should speak with someone? Perhaps not. It was not wise to let others in. Perhaps, the mature thing to do was to believe my husband was so inundated with schoolwork, he was studying into the late hours of the night; and unable to come home?"

What path should I have chosen?

☐ **Red Flag Alert:** During those months, I began to hear the gentle whisper of the Holy Spirit say, "I am your Help and your Shield." Over and over, He kept saying the same thing to me, but I tried to ignore it.

Though I knew I was hearing the voice of the Holy Spirit, how did trying to ignore it affect my spiritual battle?

☐ **Red Flag Alert:** As the days and weeks went by, I hardly ever saw my husband. After some time, I noticed some of his clothes and shoes were missing from the closet. Then I realized he was waiting for me to leave the house to come home to get some things. So many bells went off in my head, but I kept all this to myself.

Isolation is a major tool of the enemy to keep you in spiritual bondage. What should I have done?

Chapter 4

My Nightmare

For the first week or so, my husband denied it. He kept insisting he barely knew the girl. My heart was so desperate to believe the lie, and I allowed myself to believe everything was okay.

Until one day, two of my best friends came over and while we were talking, it suddenly dawned on me, "My husband was actually having an affair."

In the middle of our conversation, mid-sentence, I ran outside, got in my car, and drove like a 'mad woman' to his school. To be honest, it was a miracle I made it to his school safely. I was behind the wheel, but I was not present for the drive as I vividly remember driving in between lanes, wailing the entire time.

All the while, one of the things he had said to me was all the clothes he had been taking from the closet were in his trunk. So, when I got to his school, I made him open his trunk and lo and behold it was empty. I think it was then I realized as much as I wanted his lies to be true, they really were not.

A few days later, he came home and told me he had something to tell me.

I was sitting on our bed next to him, but before he spoke, instantly my heart knew. He went on to tell me he had slept with the girl. I asked him how many times, to which he responded,

"Once." I knew it was a lie, but I kept quiet. I asked if he kept his wedding band on, he said, "Yes."

As tears filled my eyes, when I looked at him, all I saw and felt through the tears was the love of Jesus in my heart and the price He paid on the cross. Don't ask me how. I was broken. But somehow, through it all, I saw a picture of God's forgiveness.

I opened my mouth to speak but all I heard myself say was, "I forgive you."

The rest of the night and the few days following were a blur. He pretended to be home, but I later found out he was still very much involved with the girl. After about two days of being home, he was gone again. Then, my nightmare became my new reality.

My Nightmare, My Reality

The first year, 2016-2017, was the hardest. I came to understand what David meant when he said:

> "I am worn out from sobbing. All night I flood my
> bed with weeping, drenching it with my tears."
> (Psalms 6:6 NLT)

My body began to shut down. I lost fifteen pounds in three weeks. I was a shadow of myself.

I wept, all the time. When I was not weeping, I slept. Sleeping numbed me of the pain.

I began to experience symptoms of what, in medicine, is called, "the broken heart syndrome" – *Takotsubo cardiomyopathy*. It felt like I was having a heart attack that just would not stop. My Aunt (and Pastor's wife who is also a Nurse Practitioner) wanted to take me to the hospital, but I refused.

I did not realize, at the time, that I was clinically depressed. I presented with all symptoms (listed below) to make an easy diagnosis, for many weeks on end:

- Sleep disturbance
- Lack of interest in the things once enjoyed
- Feelings of guilt and/or feelings of worthlessness
- Lack of energy
- Difficulty concentrating
- Appetite or weight changes
- Psychomotor retardation or agitation
- Passive suicidal ideations

I experienced every single one of those symptoms.

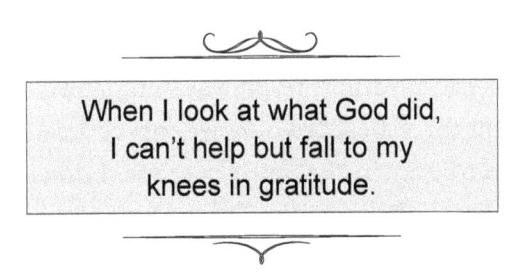

> When I look at what God did, I can't help but fall to my knees in gratitude.

While I had absolutely no desire to kill myself, more than once when I drove on the highway, I would hear the enemy whisper to me: "Why don't you just drive off the cliff? Or why don't you just drive into the forest?" Immediately, I would rebuke the enemy. I would place my hand on my head and begin to command my thoughts to align with Jesus Christ and His Word over me. I would literally say to myself, "Chiso, you have the mind of Christ, and you will think only as God commands."

My best friend lived in the U.K. and I was on the phone with her virtually every day. My other two best friends lived close by. I spent most of my time at their homes. They had little kids and I longed to just hold the kids. To someone looking in, it may have seemed like I was giving the kids hugs. However, it was quite the opposite. The kids were giving me hugs.

For a whole year, I had no desire to cook. My church family cooked for me.

I did not have the strength to buy groceries, so they bought groceries and dropped them off at my house. I had no desire to take care of my appearance and do the things I loved to do, like mani pedis, make up, etc. I just let myself be very bare. My heart was too broken to care about any of it.

All the while, at random times, I would hear the Lord say to my heart, "I am your Help and your Shield." Some days I believed it, and, on other days, it was harder to believe because the pain was excruciating. Yes, it was inundating.

I told my three best friends, whenever I call you crying, please begin to pray in the Spirit over me. I don't need words, just pray. I remember one day I found a quiet place at work, and I called them crying. For thirty minutes, I wept while they prayed over me. Afterward, I wiped my tears and went back to my desk.

At first, it was hard for me to pray. It felt like I had no strength. Yes, I would war in prayer over my husband because I realized he was in spiritual bondage, but to pray over my heart was hard.

Even though I knew where the girl lived, the Lord forbade me to go there. On more than one occasion, I tried driving there, and the Holy Spirit would literally, on my way, command me to turn around and go back home. On one of such days, I was upset and determined to go find him. But again, the Holy Spirit commanded me to turn around. So, I drove to my husband's pharmacy school instead. When I found his car, I was so angry that I wanted to drive my car into his. Yes, to crash both our cars, but the Lord restrained me.

Instead, I sat in my car staring at his car. Then, I called one of my friends weeping. I did not speak, I just wept. She began to speak God's Word over me and to encourage my heart. Finally, I got off the phone and decided to go home. On my drive home, in deep sorrow, I said to the Lord, "God, why did You allow this to happen? You could have taken my house, my car, anything at all, why did You take the one thing which mattered the most to me?"

In His still small voice, I heard Him say, "You shall have no other gods before Me. There was a reason I asked Abraham to sacrifice Isaac and not Sarah. Your husband had taken the place in your heart meant only for Me."

The rest of the drive was quiet. The dialogue ceased.

I had recently just watched the movie "War Room". Inspired by it, I turned our walk-in closet into my prayer closet. As soon as I got home, I went there to listen as the Lord continued to speak to me.

> He said, *"Yes, your husband broke My seventh commandment, "You shall not commit adultery."* (Exodus 20:14 NKJV). But you broke My first: *"I am the Lord your God, Who brought you out of the land of Egypt, out of the house of bondage. You shall have no other gods before Me."* (Exodus 20:2-3 NKJV).

You see, when I fell in love with my husband, I fell completely in love with him. He became my everything and without realizing it, I began to idolize him. While I had given my life to Jesus, repeatedly falling into sin with my husband before we got married had seared my conscience and caused my love for Jesus to grow cold. Even after the wedding, without realizing it, God was not my number one.

> *"...for I the Lord your God, am a jealous God..."*
> (Exodus 20:5 NKJV).

I listened as the Lord began to lovingly, but in no uncertain terms, speak to my heart. He began to point out the many ways I had given up the throne of my heart for the man I loved. I listened and received His loving correction.

Please, do not misunderstand me. I am in no way saying the Lord punished me with this ordeal because I idolized my husband. Rather, what I am alluding to is, amidst everything going on, God in His loving kindness and in His goodness, saw it fit to use the opportunity to point out to me areas of my life where I had gone wrong.

> *"And have you forgotten His encouraging Words spoken to you as His children? He said, "My child, don't underestimate the value of the discipline and training of the Lord God, or get depressed when He has to correct you. For the Lord's training of your life is the evidence of His faithful love. And when He draws you to Himself, it proves you are His delightful child." Fully embrace God's correction as part of your training, for He is doing what*

any loving father does for his children. For who has ever heard of a child who never had to be corrected?" (Hebrews 12:5-7 TPT)

Another translation puts it this way:

"And you have forgotten the exhortation which speaks to you as to sons: "My son, do not despise the chastening of the Lord, nor be discouraged when you are rebuked by Him; for whom the Lord loves He chastens, and scourges every son whom He receives." If you endure chastening, God deals with you as with sons; for what son is there whom a father does not chasten?"
(Hebrews 12:5-7 NKJV)

    I slept in my prayer closet that night. I repented before Jesus and invited Him to have His rightful place.
    As the days went on, I found that most nights, the floor of the closet was my bed. I fell into a revolving system – I would go to work, visit with my two friends and their kids, take naps on their couch, wake up, go back home, meet with the Lord in my closet, fall asleep there, wake up at 4:00 a.m. to be with the Lord, and then, go to work at 6:00 a.m.
    I began to pay attention to things at home because I noticed my husband would come home when I was gone to pick up more of his clothes. I had a prayer board, so I started writing out prayers for him and Bible verses on there. I would leave sticky notes all over the house with different prayers and Bible verses. Some notes on the bathroom mirror with little reminders of God's Word and others in different parts of our home.

Days turned to weeks, and he never came back home.

Most days were hard. Mainly because he was somewhat present; he gave a smidgen of his mind to our marriage when it was convenient. He would randomly call for about a minute, he would send long texts that were only drops for our deeply parched marriage. We would go back and forth, arguing about whom to blame and when he'd finally be home. He would tell me tales about how he had cut off the girl, that he was sleeping at a friend's house, and his plans of getting an apartment on campus. They were all ridden with lies.

The paucity of trust between us led me to do things unimaginable, to the detriment of my mental health. I started checking his call logs. I would wake up in the middle of the night puzzled and anxious about where he was and whom he was with. Then, I would hear a suggested whisper from the enemy, "Why don't you check his call logs." I would sit there telling myself not to. Without restraint, I would log onto our T-Mobile plan to check, and I would spend hours scrolling through his call and text logs. Expectedly, I saw all the calls he made to her and the frequency of their text communications. I had no access to the actual messages, just the logs.

Every time I checked, my heart would break all over again. It was my Pandora's box, a vicious cycle. I knew it would hurt, but I could not help checking it repeatedly. I was so engrossed and mildly obsessed that I enlisted a friend of mine to help change my password. I thought, 'if I have no knowledge of the password, I'd be protected from this habit.' Alas, that didn't prevent me. I found my way back into the account and, consequently, the habit.

Looking back now, I realize that I always went back with the hope that the status quo changed. No, it never changed.

Another thing I had to endure were the endless "trolls" from the girls he was with. On many occasions, they sent me texts informing me that my husband was going to divorce me. How they got my number is still a mystery. That one hurt; a whole lot. Those texts were precursors to panic attacks. My default response would be to call a friend and we'd stay on the call until I was successfully calmed.

I felt exposed. It felt like someone had broken into my home and removed my "covering." All the while, I was still expected to function at work and lead a normal life. Indeed, I was angry; very angry. However, I knew I could not act on my anger. I had no choice but to share my emotions with my friends and prayer partners.

One night, I was so upset, I went to my church building, and I decided to spend the night in the church sanctuary. I was going to stay awake through the night to question God and He was going to answer me. (I'm cringing as I write this…)

I began my vent:

> *Lord, why did You give me this man?!*
> *I was not looking for marriage and I certainly did not ask for this man!*
> *Why, Lord, did You bring this trouble to me? I was perfectly fine on my own!*
> *I was minding my own business when You said he was my husband!*
> *So, WHY, Lord?!*

On and on I went, livid. Through tears, I demanded a response from the Lord.

The first hour went by.

Midway through the second hour, I fell asleep. It was only about 1:00 a.m. So much for my vigil :)

In the morning, I went home and continued to fight for my marriage. I quickly realized: 'God is on my side. He is for me'. So, I intentionally set my heart to cling to Jesus.

However, it was difficult to read God's Word. Not because I was angry at Him, but the weight of it all was immense. Once, my friends and their spouses all got on the phone and began to read the book of Psalms over me. We must have read through twenty chapters. We did not discuss any of it, we simply took turns reading a chapter and moving on to the next chapter.

These verses ministered to me:

> *"The Spirit gives life; the flesh counts for nothing. The words I have spoken to you - they are full of the Spirit and life."* (John 6:63 NIV)

> *"For the Word of God is living and active and full of power [making it operative, energizing, and effective]. It is sharper than any two-edged sword, penetrating as far as the division of the soul and spirit [the completeness of a person], and of both joints and marrow [the deepest parts of our nature], exposing and judging the very thoughts and intentions of the heart."* (Hebrews 4:12 AMP)

As we all read together, the Lord began to wash over me with His Word and to cause strength to rise in me. His Word began to bring life to every dead and discouraged part of my heart. Little by little, the Lord began to strengthen me. Through this process, He gave me the strength to go back to reading His Word on my own.

> "He gives power to the weak, and to those who have no might He increases strength. Even the youths shall faint and be weary, and the young men shall utterly fall, but those who wait on the Lord shall renew their strength; they shall mount up with wings like eagles, they shall run and not be weary, they shall walk and not faint."
> (Isaiah 40:29-31 NKJV)

The more I sought Him, the more I leaned on Him. I literally could not function without Jesus. For my dear life, I held on to Him. The Lord was so faithful in His love. It felt like He put a covering as a shield over my heart and did not allow the pain of it to crush me. He kept me busy. He led me to immerse myself in His business. Worship practice, I was there. Bible study nights, I was there. Evangelism days, count me present. For my sanity, I had to be intentional about my time and what I allowed in my heart.

About two months into this, through a conversation with my husband's younger sister, ironically, the Lord led me to go back to school to study medicine. My rationale was that my mind needed a distraction. He laid on my heart the desire to pursue admission to a Physician Associate (PA) Program.

Honestly, taking the prerequisites was just something I did with no expectation of getting accepted into a program. Simply because if you know anything about PA programs, you know the chances of getting in are beyond slim. I am talking on average ~3000 competitive applicants for 32 seats. I took the courses anyway because it gave my mind something to focus on.

Strangely enough, sitting in the prerequisite classes drew my heart closer to Jesus.

One day, I remember sitting in an Anatomy and Physiology class, learning about the body's respiratory mechanism. To hone in on his point, my professor explained how a part of our brain – *the medulla* – reminds us to breathe every three seconds. And I thought to myself, "Just in case I forget, God is making sure my body breathes?!"

Next, we talked about the heart and how everything must work properly to keep me alive. I saw the structure of the heart and I was struck by how small it is for all its responsibilities. Again, I thought to myself, "The Lord of the universe dutifully holds my heart in His hands?!" I was speechless!

Throughout my prerequisites, the Lord overwhelmed me with excellence and favor. Exam after exam, I kept getting A's. I would get my test results and simply get on my knees in awe of and grateful to the Lord. "How was this all possible?", I wondered. My world was literally upside down, yet He gave me understanding beyond what I could ever have imagined possible.

Right around my final exams, I saw some things on my husband's phone (details to come in subsequent chapters), and I lost it. I loaded up my car with everything in my suitcases and I left. Well, he pulled into the garage right as I was pulling out and he decided to come after me. So, we had a little race on the highway (I laugh now at the foolishness of it all, but nothing about it was funny at the time). Needless to say, I was not able to study as I normally would. All I could do was listen to lecture recordings. In despair, I thought to myself, "I am going to have to drop this final exam grade." After the exam, I was walking by and my professor saw me and said to me, "Chiso, you got a perfect score, a 100%."

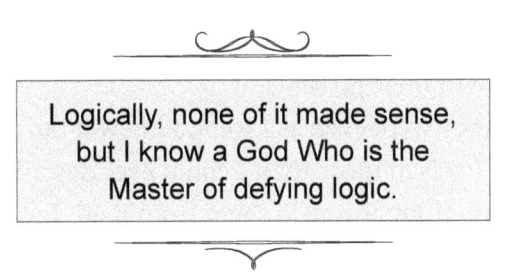

> Logically, none of it made sense, but I know a God Who is the Master of defying logic.

Family Support

There is one piece of this I am yet to talk about – my family. Ranked second to my relationship with Jesus is the one I nurture with my family. They mean more to me than anything or anyone else. Our parents raised us to be close knit, hence, we share everything with one another. As a result, this was the hardest part to face, and I kept the bulk of the pain from them for a period for two reasons:

1. I knew they would be devastated and a part of me desperately wanted to shelter them from the pain. So, I acted like everything was okay for about two months after it all began before finally letting them in.
2. My husband was not just an in-law to them. He had become their son and brother. The thought of severing their relationship and the damage it would cause was too great to face, especially because I was trusting the Lord to bring healing and restoration.

The Calm in My Storm

Nevertheless, I finally opened up to them a few months after everything began, in August 2016. Shortly after I told them, my mom and siblings came over to be with me. It was such a comfort having them around. Even without knowing the extent of what I was experiencing, they were holding me up not just in prayer but with their presence.

I knew they wept even as I wept. I knew it hurt them to see all the pain I was in more than I could ever describe. If I could have done anything to shield them from it all, I would have.

Periodically, I kept back some of the details of how much pain I was in. By doing so, though, I did not realize how difficult it was for them. They wanted to share in the burden of my pain, but I denied them.

My older self would advise my younger self to do things differently and allow them to be there for me in every way I needed them. This is why God created families.

Now, I know better.

———✻———

My Nightmare

Red Flag Alerts

As you continue this journey with me through my marital trials, pause and reflect on the Red Flag Alerts I failed to recognize or did not heed. Review this chapter and consider how you might have done things differently if you encountered a similar situation.

Red Flag Alert: When I fell in love with my husband, he became my everything. I began to idolize him. Falling into sin with my husband before we got married had seared my conscience and caused my love for Jesus to grow cold. After the wedding, without realizing it, God was not my number one.

Read Exodus 20:5.

> *What did idolizing my husband do to my relationship with God?*
>
> *Examine your life and ask God to reveal any areas where you have created an idol. Repent immediately!*

Red Flag Alert: My older self would advise my younger self to do things differently and allow them to be there for me in every way I needed them.

Have you shut your family and friends out of certain areas of your life thinking you are protecting them from pain?
What did you learn from reading my life experience?

Red Flag Alert: The paucity of trust between us led me to do things unimaginable, to the detriment of my mental health. I started checking his call logs.

Whose "voice" was I listening to?

Whose voice should I have been listening to?

Whose voice have you been listening to?

If it is not God through His Holy Spirit, what do you need to do?

Chapter 5

The Psalms

Have you ever looked back on a difficult season of your life and fondly remembered the lifeline that carried you through it? Well, mine was the book of Psalms. I am still not sure how God did it. I mean, I have known about this book of the Bible all my life, it just was never one of the books that stood out to me in that way. However, the Lord led me to this book.

Each day, notifications streamed into my phone, some from my husband and others from girls he was with, or their friends. They would tell me how my husband was getting ready to divorce me. Over and over, I received those messages. Messages from my husband were incendiary.

Red Flag Alert: Each time, I would read messages that distracted and disturbed me. Sometimes, they came late at night, and they left me anxious, making me fall asleep with nightmares. And, waking up from those nightmares would immediately set my day on a bad course.

> **News from gossiping friends
> is bad news.
> Stop listening. Turn it off.
> Listen to God.
> The only news He has for you
> is Good News!**

So, the Lord in His goodness gave me a nightly routine.

First, He gave me the wisdom to mute my text and call notifications at the end of the day. Those on my favorite list – my family, my best friends, and some praying partners – were whitelisted, they could still call me. However, everyone else was sentineled.

Next, God would lead me into His presence and sit me down to speak to my heart. He made sure that the last Person I interacted with and the last thought on my mind before bed was Him. That helped me fall asleep in His peace and not have nightmares about what my husband was or was not doing.

Then, in the morning, before reading any message or entertaining anything else from the noise of the world, the Lord, the Good Shepherd, comforted me and spoke peace to my anxious heart and mind. Beginning with the first chapter of Psalms, God and I read through; chapter-by-chapter, night after night. And, as I read through, miraculous things happened.

> *"You will keep him in perfect peace,*
> *Whose mind is stayed on You,*
> *Because he trusts in You.*

> *Trust in the Lord forever,*
> *For in Yah, the Lord, is everlasting strength."*
> (Isaiah 26:3-4 NKJV)

The word "stayed", in this verse, means fixed and focused. Have you ever had someone who simply stared you down until you asked, "What do you want? Do you need something from me?" That's the way it is when your total focus—body, mind and soul—is on the Lord God. Fix your eyes on Jesus, the Author and Perfecter of your faith. Your strength is in the Lord when you put your total trust in and gaze on Him.

> *"The Word of God is living and powerful, and sharper than any two-edged sword, piercing even to the division of soul and spirit, and of joints and marrow, and is a discerner of the thoughts and intents of the heart."* (Hebrews 4:12 NKJV)

His Word to me as I read through the pages of the book of Psalms were like a surgeon's scalpel. God surgically removed every lying thought and negative feeling in me, replacing them with the healing balm of His truth, comfort, and peace.

While I know the earlier stated verse of Hebrews 4:12 has a myriad of interpretations, the Lord ministered it to me thus: *'My Word is perfectly powerful to the point of piercing through all the pain you are in and reaching deep down to the depths of your soul. And, as My Word goes in, it is speaking life to your very heart.'*

So, as I read His Word, He began to heal my heart. God *"sent out His Word and healed them, snatching them from the door of death."* (Psalm 107:20 NLT).

I wish I could describe with words what He did but I do not have the vocabulary to do so because it was all mystical.

When in troubling circumstances and losing your way, do what?

Through this process, the Lord opened my eyes to a secret. You see, David was a man in the Bible who, while he was called "a man after God's own heart", he had an immense number of ups and downs in his life. And, through them all, he would always run to the Lord. Reading through the Psalms showed me how, in one verse or chapter, David would start by lamenting his circumstance, and, in the next, remind his heart of the goodness of the Lord. For instance:

> *"Lord, how my foes increase! There are many who attack me. Many say about me, 'there is no help for him in God.' But You, Lord, are a shield around me, my glory and the One Who lifts up my head."* (Psalms 3:1-3 CSB)

Again:

> *"My tears have been my food day and night, while all day long people say to me, 'Where is your God?'... The Lord will send His faithful love by day, His song will be with me in the night - a prayer to the God of my life."* (Psalms 42:3 & 8 CSB)

And again:

> *"Why, my soul, are you so dejected? Why are you in such turmoil? Put your hope in God, for I will still praise Him, my Savior, and my God. I am deeply depressed; therefore, I remember You..."* (Psalms 42:5-6 CSB)

At some time, David was afraid and felt like his bad season would never end:

> *"My whole being is shaken with terror. And You, Lord - how long?... Depart from me, all evildoers, for the Lord has heard the sound of my weeping. The Lord has heard my plea for help; the Lord accepts my prayer."* (Psalms 6:3, 8-9 CSB)

At other times, he'd acknowledge his despair and *choose* to praise louder:

> *""Lord my God, I seek refuge in You; save me from all my pursuers and rescue me, or they will tear me like a lion, ripping me apart with no one to rescue me."... "Lord, our Lord, how magnificent is Your name throughout the earth! You have covered the heavens with Your majesty.""*
> (Psalms 7:1-2, 8:1 CSB)

Sometimes, his heart would be a little more discouraged and he would pour that out to the Lord also:

> *"How long, Lord? Will You forget me forever? How long will You hide Your face from me? How long will I store up anxious concerns within me, agony in my mind every day? How long will my enemy dominate me?... But I have trusted in Your faithful love; my heart will rejoice in Your deliverance. I will sing to the Lord because He has treated me generously."* (Psalms 13:1-2, 5-6 CSB)

Some other times, David would be more confident and go on praising the Lord:

> *"Lord, You are my portion and my cup of blessing; You hold my future. The boundary lines have fallen for me in pleasant places; indeed, I have a beautiful inheritance. I will bless the Lord Who counsels me - even at night when my thoughts trouble me. I know the Lord is always with me, I will not be shaken, for He is right beside me. Therefore my heart is glad and my whole being rejoices; my body also rests securely. For You will not abandon me to Sheol; You will not allow Your faithful one to see decay."*
> (Psalms 16:5-10, CSB and NLT)

Ultimately, an entire chapter and my all-time favorite Psalm – Psalm 18 – grounded me and ministered to me His mercy, grace, peace, and comfort.

What Reading the Psalms Taught Me

If I were to write about all that the Lord did through the book of Psalms, I won't stop writing until His return. The point is, He showed me a mystery: the heart that dares to dig a little deeper and go beyond seeing the Psalms as *just poems*, would learn the secret and discover one of the greatest spiritual arsenals in the kingdom of God: the ability to rise above what you see in the physical and choose instead to declare the victory of God over every circumstance. In doing so, He used it to rescue my soul from my deepest anguish.

And, as I read and fell in love with the book of Psalms, the Lord taught me to fight just like David fought, tears and pain notwithstanding.

Next, He gave me this:

> *"Do you not know? Have you not heard? The Lord is the everlasting God, the Creator of the ends of the earth. He will not grow tired or weary, and* ***His understanding no one can fathom.***"
> (Isaiah 40:28 NIV)

I am not quite sure how to explain the gift of this verse to me, but I will try.

In a season where I was more than surrounded by family, friends, church community who all loved me so much, the Lord showed me that He, even He, the Creator God, the One Who spoke the world into being, the Master of the universe and the Mighty God, fully understood my pain. He understood the depth of it. Not just that. He showed me that, try as I might, I could never fully grasp the depth of His understanding of my hurt. The knowledge of this comforted my heart and reassured me of His ever-abiding presence. Armed with all this, I played the waiting game regarding my marriage.

Different prophecies came forth about the Lord restoring my marriage by the end of August 2016. And as the calendar turned to September 1st, 2016, and my husband was still not home, my heart sank. But, as I had come to learn to do, I went back to the Lord for comfort, and I continued to rely on my community of family, friends, and church family.

Towards the end of September 2016, by some miracle, my husband agreed to marital counseling. You can imagine my joy. Not only would I get to see him in person, but we would also have a chance to talk things through and arrive at a solution. Even with this, I had doubts. Would he show up or would he come up with an excuse at the last minute?

To my shock, he showed up.

The counselor gave us some take-home assignments. I remember after one session, my husband came home so we could complete the assignments together. It seemed like we were starting to connect again. Alas, at the end of it, he stood up and told me he was going back to "his apartment."

During the sessions, I implored the counselor to explain to him the need to come home so we could work on the marriage from inside the home. To which he replied, he did not feel comfortable coming home until he was done with an exam he had coming up and until we had resolved things. *Seriously?!* What well-intentioned and sane couple would choose to fix their marriage by living in different homes?! Honestly, make it make sense….

Red Flag Alert: On one of the nights after completing the take-home assignment, he offered to take me to see this "apartment" of his to prove to me that he was really living in his own place. He took me to what I would call a "room" on campus that had maybe three or four of his personal items, a bed, and a bathroom. I took one look at the place, saw how tidy it was and knew that there was no way on earth the man I married and lived with for some time was residing in this clean and well put together room. And, in that moment, just when I thought he could not possibly have any more part of my heart left to break, he succeeded in breaking my heart all over again because I wondered: *what on earth would cause a man who said he loved me and vowed in front of 500+ people to be mine to stoop so low as to stage a fake apartment just so I would not catch him in a lie and he could continue living with another girl?!*

> "Hope deferred makes the heart sick,
> but a longing fulfilled is a tree of life."
> (Proverbs 13:12 NIV)

After that night, and 3 or 4 counseling sessions into our program, I decided I was no longer going to waste my time attending the sessions, trying to make peace with a man that was still living with another woman. So, I stopped.

In the weeks and months that followed, he and I kept in touch infrequently, mostly via text. He said all the right things that made him look like the victim. In the most basic form, it was very manipulative. He would sound like he was coming around, but then he would continue to live outside. On my end, I had to keep praying and holding on to faith that the Lord would bring him back to me. My typical prayer line was as follows: *Father, please restore my husband first to You and second to me.* I understood that if my husband could get back to seeing Jesus, the Lord would redirect his heart to me and restore our marriage. So, with my heart in its most shattered state, I continued to pray. On some days I felt like giving up. On other days I was strengthened and encouraged to continue to persevere.

One other thing I really struggled with was shame. *"Above all, lift up the [protective] shield of faith with which you can extinguish all the flaming arrows of the evil one."* (Ephesians 6:16 AMP)

Handling Shame

Red Flag Alert: Somehow, the enemy managed to convince me to be ashamed. He had designed specific arrows for me, and he was throwing them with all his might. Some of the lies he spoke to my heart were:

- *"You were unable to keep your husband, so he left"*
- *"You cannot even keep a marriage together. Look around at your friends and everyone else with their spouses, some of them already have their kids and here you are with your husband running the streets."*
- *"Look, there is someone else who knows that your husband has left you"*
- *"Everyone knows and they are mocking and laughing at you"*
- *"Woe is you"*

Incessantly, he brought one condemning thought after another. It was a constant barrage. And I was afraid. I was mostly terrified of people (who did not know what was going on) finding out that as much as I tried to put on a brave face, my husband was not home. So, whenever people would ask where he was, I would do this weird thing of acting like they were asking about my heavenly Bridegroom – Jesus. My response, thereafter, would be "He is home". Madness, I know, ha-ha. But the heart can sometimes convince the mind to hold on to something even when it knows it to be untrue. So, I went along with my cover.

All the while feeling inadequate, unwanted, and unloved by my husband. Leaving me very exposed. I also found that more men were hitting on me when my husband was gone. It was strange but it felt like the covering that comes by virtue of the husband's presence was taken away and I was 'vulnerable' in many ways. Thankfully, the Lord shielded me and reminded me that He is and always will be my covering.

I was also under tremendous financial strain. All the bills fell on me: rent, our phone bills, car notes for both his car and mine, utility bills, the purchase of the groceries, veterinary bills for our dog, etc. He lived as he wished, shirking his responsibilities. Therefore, as distressed as I was, I also had the unenviable task of working to keep our affairs afloat financially.

A month later, on the weekend of November 5th, I went to New York to be with my sister for her birthday. On Sunday November 6th, we were in the middle of a service at Hillsong NYC church when I got a text from my husband. I have forgotten exactly what he said but I knew something was up. I got back to Maryland that night to find that, after seven months of being gone, my husband had finally come home. Was I facing a coming train wreck or a possible healing in our marriage?

The Psalms

Red Flag Alerts

As you continue this journey with me through my marital trials, pause and reflect on the Red Flag Alerts I failed to recognize or did not heed. Review this chapter and consider how you might have done things differently if you encountered a similar situation.

Red Flag Alert: Each time, I would read messages that distracted and disturbed me. Sometimes, they came late at night, and they left me anxious, making me fall asleep with nightmares. And, waking up from those nightmares would immediately set my day on a bad course.

I was distracted by what everyone around me was telling me about my bad circumstances. When you have problems and issues, to whom do you go for wise advice and counsel?

Red Flag Alert: On one of the nights after completing the take-home assignment, he offered to take me to see this "apartment" of his to prove to me that he was really living in his own place. He took me to what I would call a "room" on campus that had maybe three or four of his personal items, a bed, and a bathroom. I took one look at the place, saw how tidy it was and knew that there was no way on earth the man I married and lived with for some time was residing in this clean and well put together room. And, in that moment, just when I thought he could not possibly have any more part of my heart left to break, he succeeded in breaking my heart all over again because I wondered: *what on earth would cause a man who said he loved me and vowed in front of 500+ people to be mine to stoop so low as to stage a fake apartment just so I would not catch him in a lie and he could continue living with another girl?!*

When a spouse, family member or friend is lying to you and manipulating you, what keeps you focused on the Truth…what is God saying to you?

Red Flag Alert: The enemy was attacking me with shame.

When you feel shame and self-condemnation, what does the truth of Scripture tell you about God's forgiving love?

Chapter 6

The Dream

His sudden return home left me with many questions.

- *What is happening?*
- *After seven long months, why has he chosen to return home?!*
- *Is this real? Or is my imagination playing tricks on me?*
- *Have I longed for this day so dearly that it's happening not in the exact way I wanted and desired it?*

That evening, we sat at the dining table, and I asked some of these questions. He told me he desired to be at home and wanted nothing more with the girl, that he had cut her off completely and wanted to make things right with us. I believed him; at least my heart did. However, something seemed off, but I willed my mind to dismiss it. I remember seeing tears stream down his face as he told me he was completely done with her. I tried desperately to hold on to what that could mean. But I still could not shake the feeling that something was amiss.

A few hours into the evening, he fell asleep on the couch. And, as soon as he slept off, I reached for his Mac computer and saw that just before he went to bed, he had sent two messages to the same number:

Her: Wya? *(meaning 'where you at')*
Him: (I do not recall his response to her)
Him: Wyd? *(meaning 'what you doing')*

When I saw the name of the person he was chatting with, my heart sank.

Everything he had spent the past few hours telling me was a lie, all of it. What was my crime? What was so wrong in loving someone so much that I had to keep getting slapped in the face?

Red Flag Alert: A potential restoration now seemed further away than ever.

When you need to confront someone with the truth, what are the right, godly steps to take? Are there ways to say the right words, in God's way, at the right time, in humility, without judgment or anger? Is that even possible? Absolutely!

- *Speak the truth in love.*
- *Be quick to listen, slow to speak, and slow to anger.*
- *Refuse to be offended and ready to forgive.*
- *Understand that true repentance is to admit it, quit it, and then forget it.*

If the person hurting you both admits their wrongs and then quits doing them, that person has turned away from their sin.

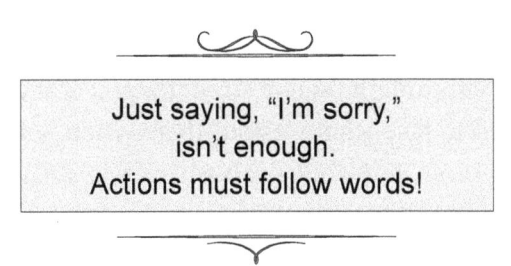

> Just saying, "I'm sorry,"
> isn't enough.
> Actions must follow words!

In the day(s) to follow, I would later find out that he and the girl had gotten into an argument, and she had kicked him out of her apartment. So, his return home was not because he was "done", as he so deceptively put it. Rather, she had sent him packing and, since he had nowhere else to go, he came home.

Red Flag Alert: They were still seeing each other; they just were not living together anymore. His manipulation and deception were still at work. I was hoping for true repentance and a change of heart and actions from him. Would that ever happen?

> *"Not getting what you want can break your heart,
> but a wish that comes true is a life-giving tree"*
> (Proverbs 13:12 CEV)

Living with my Husband was Chaotic.

I was not prepared for all the challenges that would come with having him under the same roof. For example, he would stay out late until the early hours of the morning and only come home when I was fast asleep. He refused to sleep in our bed, so the living room was his room and the couch his bed.

I learned to not step out of our bedroom in the mornings until I had gone to my prayer closet to commune with the Lord.

I would sit with the Lord and ask Him for strength. He would endow me with unfathomable strength, grace, and everything else I needed to face what was out there. Then, I would go out to the living room and while my husband was still asleep on the couch, I would kiss him on his forehead, whisper to him that I loved him and head out to work.

I would come home from work only to find our living room very untidy and disorganized. He would leave his clothes all over the house: on the floor, on the couch, on the stairs, you name it. So, when I got home and he was out, I would pick up his clothes, launder them; take out his dirty dishes with stale morsels from the living room, wash them; and pick up everything else after him.

Red Flag Alert: As I cleaned up after him, his clothes would reek of cigarette smoke. The first time I smelt it, my heart further broke. The man I married was not a smoker. And while I could not tell whether the smoke was from him or from the environment he had been in, it all still hurt. Nevertheless, the Lord wiped my tears, and I would keep on cleaning until everything was back in order. The next day, I would get home from work to find his "living area" right back to being messy. And, again, I would clean up. I thought that my lovingkindness would bring a breakthrough. It was exhausting. But my mind was set on loving him back to his "senses".

Some days, it was merely perfunctory. Other days, I struggled to keep up. But the Lord was my strength. He never left my side. So, for as long as I could, I kept doing it.

However, one morning, I woke up a little earlier than planned and I walked downstairs, after being with the Lord, only to find my husband looking at what I assumed was her photo on his phone and masturbating*. In all the time of being with my husband, I had NEVER seen him masturbate or known that to be something he ever struggled with.

> *Please note, I share this incident with no intention to shame or defame him but rather to explain to you, the reader, the extent to which sin can transform a person's life and the extent to which the enemy will go to destroy a person when he or she opens the door to sexual perversion. In the blink of an eye, sin can transform a minister of the Gospel to someone completely unrecognizable. As Proverbs puts it "Can a man scoop a flame into his lap and not have his clothes catch on fire?" (Proverbs 6:27 NLT)

I was so startled I let out a yelp, began to weep, and ran back upstairs to my prayer closet.

- *I believed that it was God's will for us to stay together and for my husband to repent and return to his senses like the prodigal son.*
- *I believed that God could do the "seemingly" impossible.*
- *I believed that my husband could change. However, nothing I did brought him around. My ultimate recourse was prayer.*

I spent a lot of time weeping and in prayer. I cried repeatedly until I had nothing left to pour out. I was angry. I wanted to give up on him. I wanted, so desperately, to be done with all of it.

I sent texts to my friends letting them know the hurt I had just witnessed, and they encouraged me with God's Word. But frankly, my heart was really hurting. It felt so unfair. And I was left with many more questions:

Why?
Why me?
Why did this have to be my cross to bear?

I was beginning to learn that my *Why* questions were going unanswered. The *When* and *What* and *How* questions, too. The only question that got an answer was *Who I could trust*. Not him…not even myself or others…only Christ.

Often, I would think back to the man I met almost a decade ago, the same man who became my best friend before he became my husband. Where was that man? Where had he gone? I just wanted him to come home to me, to really come home. I was not asking for someone else's husband, Lord, I just wanted mine back. Was that too much to ask? And how could a person change so much in such a short amount of time?

Amidst all the questions and the hurt, I would still find reasons to hold on to him and to our marriage. I would say to myself: *Chiso, if the roles were reversed and you were the one who strayed, he would fight for you.* And so, I stayed and kept on fighting for him and for us.

A few days later, I got a hold of his cellphone and saw a conversation between him and the girl. When he realized I had his phone, he and I got entangled in quite a tussle for it. We both fell to the ground. I fell awkwardly on my hip and got hurt; but I could not even think about that. I was so upset, I cursed at him. I used a vulgar word that the Lord will not permit me to repeat, nor would I want to ever utter again.

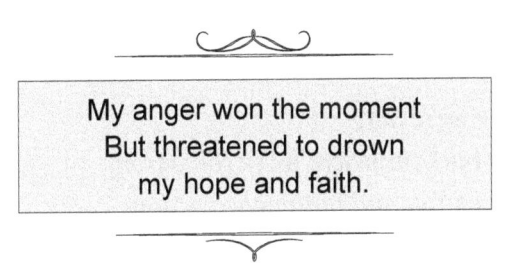

> My anger won the moment
> But threatened to drown
> my hope and faith.

I told my friends what transpired. And, as always, they encouraged me with God's Word and reminded me to trust in Jesus Christ.

Would God Make a Way?

Life went on like this with him until one night he left and did not come home. The next morning, I remember lying in bed listening to "Made a Way" by Travis Greene when he walked into the house. He went into our bedroom closet but did not realize I was in the room, on the bed. He was on the phone telling the person on the other end about the previous night and all he did. I kept quiet and listened. Eventually, he turned around, saw me, and ended the conversation.

As usual, I had a crying session that morning. As I cried, the Holy Spirit held me close to His heart. At the same time, the words to the song kept playing:

"...You made a way
When our backs were against the wall
And it looked as if it was over

You made a way
And we're standing here
Only because You made a way
You made a way

And now we're here
Looking back on where we've come from
Because of You and nothing we've done
To deserve the love and mercy You've shown
But Your grace was strong enough to pick us up..."

And for some reason, the Lord in His goodness chose that exact moment, when all looked bleak, to sing loudly to my heart and remind me that His grace is strong enough to pick me up. In that moment, it sounded as though the Lord was declaring in His sovereignty that even though my back was "against the wall", He was going to pick not just me but 'us' up. I held on to that word in faith. And I continued to draw strength and lean on the Lord, my family, and my community of friends and believers.

> When going through trials,
> We need the prayers and
> support of other Christian friends.
> We are never alone. God and His
> people are always there.

A Volcanic Explosion of Anger

A few days later, during a conversation between his parents and I, I divulged our state of affairs. They decided to come to our home one night, without telling my husband, to see for themselves and have a conversation with him. They got to the house and waited.

10:00 p.m. turned to 11:00 p.m.
11:00 p.m. became midnight.
Midnight turned to 1:00 a.m.
And then he came home.

To his chagrin, he walked into the house to find his mom and dad in the living room. They began to talk to him and to ask him a bunch of questions. I retreated to our bedroom. Few minutes into their conversation, things got heated. I came back out and somehow, amid all the chaos, I managed to get a hold of his cellphone.

Red Flag Alert: *What I saw both scared and scarred me.*

It took only but one conversation for me to snap. It was a conversation between my husband and a close friend of his - his best man at our wedding. The gist of it was that his friend asked him about another random girl, to which he responded and alluded to some relations with her. His exact words I do not recall. Then, the conversation switched to the friend asking him if he was going to choose me, his wife or the girl he had been having an affair with for the past couple of months. He was unsure of his position; he then went on to compare the both of us and, in essence, weigh *the pros and cons.* After which, his friend advised him to pick one woman and stick with his choice.

Again, my heart felt like it was being ripped from my chest.

You see, this whole time, I knew he was having an affair. But I saw the girl as nothing more than that. Not that that made it okay. But you must understand, in my mind, I categorized her as the inconsequential fling she was. So, to see that conversation on his phone and then to see a second girl in the picture and to see how casually he was discussing being with multiple women, it was more than I could bear.

While I looked through his phone, he was trying to get into the room to get it back. And as soon as I saw the conversations, I lost every ounce of self-control I had been holding on to for the past seven months.

I went into the hallway, and I started hitting him. I let every punch and kick fly even getting him right in his private parts. As I hit him, I screamed every kind of obscenity at him and cursed everything about him. He just stood there and took all of it. He kept telling me how sorry he was, but I was not having it. After one or two blows and kicks down there, he knew to protect his private part. But everything else he let land on him. I was hysterical.

It was sometime around 3:00 a.m., but I couldn't care less. I screamed at the top of my lungs, and I cursed him. When I was done, I ran out of the house, and he came running after me. We ran all the way to the field by our house, and I continued to yell at him. He got on his knees and began to tell me how sorry he was. But I was not having it. I told him I was done, and he told me he was done with all the women but again I was not falling for any of his lies. It was a full-on neighborhood show that night and it went on until about 5:00 a.m.

He finally convinced me to come back to the house and we both fell asleep on our bed sometime around 6:00 a.m. I woke up six hours later, and he was not in bed nor was he home. I called my friends and Pastor's wife and told them everything that had transpired the previous night. After speaking with them, I decided I was indeed done. So, I grabbed some clothes, shoes, important documents, and other essential items and loaded up my car. Just as I was pulling out of the garage, my husband was pulling into the driveway. He took one look into my car, saw that it was loaded up with my personal items, and realized I was leaving.

I Finally Left My Husband

He tried to get me to stop the car, but I refused. So, he decided he was not letting me leave. Next, we got into a car chase on the highway. Me, in my (humble :)) Toyota Corolla, and him, in his Nissan Maxima. As you can imagine, we sped past speed limits and defied traffic laws like a bunch of maniacs. Yes, it was as crazy as it sounds.

At first, I had intended to drive to my parents' home, but my parents were in Nigeria at the time, my brothers were in different countries also and my sisters were in New York. So, I did not want to drive home and be stuck there with him alone. So, I just kept driving hoping I had enough gas in my car to take me however far this chase would go.

I sent a text to my best friend in England and then sent a text to the group chat with my other friends here in the U.S., their husbands, a very dear friend of mine who had also been my husband's accountability partner/mentor, my pastor and pastor's wife. I informed them that my darling husband and I were involved in an intense car chase on the highway.

Everyone started scrambling.

My pastor's wife and my friends' husbands rushed to their respective cars to drive to where I was. We could not figure out where to go, so they told me to drive to our church. At some point, two things happened. One, my husband got into a minor "accident" with another car. Two, he must have realized what direction I was driving in and figured out that I was more than likely to have reinforcements waiting for me at church and wisely decided he did not want to follow me there. So, he let me go. I ended up going to one of my best friend's house. And, later that evening, on December 3rd, 2016, I moved my things back into my parents' home.

Red Flag Alert: One of the reasons I moved out, aside from the obvious with everything I saw on his phone, was that I no longer recognized myself. The words and language that had come out of my mouth, three weeks prior to the car chase incident and the night before the chase, were foreign to even the unsaved version of me. Hearing them come out of my mouth signaled my need to create the necessary distance. In that state, with how troubled I was, I was not in the right frame of mind to continue praying for his restoration nor the restoration of our marriage.

So, I left, and I stayed away.

The very next day, on December 4th, 2016, I remember sitting at my dining table alone in the house and thinking about everything that had transpired. The more I thought about it, more anger welled up in me. And within a few moments, I made the executive decision to take it out on myself.

It was 8:50 p.m. when I sent a text to my friends that I was about to cut off all my hair. They tried to call me, in a bid to convince me otherwise, however, I turned off my phone after I sent the text. Next, I grabbed the nearest pair of scissors and without paying attention to what I was doing, with no rhyme nor reason to my method, and with tears streaming down my face, I chopped it all off.

> Venting all my anger on myself was wrong;
> God was forgiving me,
> but in that moment,
> I couldn't forgive myself.

An hour later, at 9:50 p.m., I sent them a photo with a text saying it was done. A few minutes later, they called me on FaceTime, and they could not believe what they saw. It was an uneven cut and it looked like a hot mess. But they kept their composure and tried to find words to comfort me. The next morning, I called my best friend in England, and she was also appalled. That morning one of them called the closest barber shop and made an appointment for me.

That day, I wore a wig to work.

When I got off, I went straight to the barber shop for my appointment. I remember pulling up at the shop and feeling like scum. I sat in the chair; the barber took one look at me confused and with a question "what happened?" I could not find the words. He asked me if it had anything to do with a man and I responded *"yes, my husband."* He told me it was going to be okay. He then said that because of how bad it was, with patches in different places, he would have to shave it all off down to my scalp. I agreed to his proposed strategy and sat there while he worked. When he was done, there wasn't a stubble of hair left on my head.

Afterwards, I met up with my friends at one of their houses. To say that they were shocked does not quite do it justice. But again, they comforted me. Later, that night, I went home, took a shower, and stared at myself in the mirror. I could not recognize the person looking back at me.

Not only had I lost so much weight, but I now also looked like a boy. That was the lowest point for me. I began to cry. The more I stared, the more painful it was.

When I was done, I wiped my tears and went to sleep.

The next morning, I got dressed for work and before I left the house, the Lord knowing exactly how I was feeling, stopped me in my tracks. He had me stand in front of the mirror to look at myself. As I stared at my head seeing only my scalp, I heard my mouth begin to speak:

Chiso, you are beautifully and wonderfully made.
You are precious in God's sight, and He loves you.
This does not define you.
For you are the apple of His eye and He calls you beautiful.

I wish I could tell you I believed the words I spoke, but that would be a lie.

As far as I was concerned, I looked hideous, and I lost all sense of hope and purpose for my life.

Yet, the Holy Spirit would not let me remain in that place of despair. So, He made the voices of my family and the rest of my faith community loud in my heart and He used them to remind me of my identity and my worth.

I continued the new routine He enforced on me; I would repeatedly stand in front of the mirror and declare His Word over my entire being, the physical, the emotional, and the spiritual. I sought out verses that reminded me of how beautiful I was to Him and how He saw me. And I would speak His Words repeatedly before leaving my house to convince myself that I was not ugly. He and I did this repeatedly until we had said it often enough for my mind and my heart to believe it.

My husband came by my parents' house every now and again, and most of our conversations were heated. But I was getting stronger spiritually and feeling better emotionally. I finally felt like I was doing okay.

On December 25th, 2016, everything changed.

The Dream

Red Flag Alerts

As you continue this journey with me through my marital trials, pause and reflect on the Red Flag Alerts I failed to recognize or did not heed. Review this chapter and consider how you might have done things differently if you encountered a similar situation.

Red Flag Alert: A potential restoration now seemed further away than ever.

He told me he wanted to be at home and that he wanted nothing more with the girl. He told me he had cut her off completely and wanted to make things right with us. I believed him; at least my heart did. But I still could not shake the feeling that something was off.

- Even when your emotions try to get you to believe one thing, remember that if you belong to Jesus, He speaks to you, and you hear His voice. He gives you discernment and He will always reveal the truth to you.

- What truth has the Lord been trying to reveal to you that you have been ignoring for your own pleasure or desires?

It is never wise to ignore His still small voice.

Red Flag Alert: They were still seeing each other; they just were not living together anymore. His manipulation and deception were still at work. I was hoping for true repentance and a change of heart and actions from him. Would that ever happen?

- *True repentance will always be evident; it will be backed by fruit.*
- *For what areas of your life have you told God you are sorry only to find that you go right back to the same things you repented of?*

Red Flag Alert: As I cleaned up after him, his clothes would reek of cigarette smoke. The first time I smelt it, my heart further broke. The man I married was not a smoker. And while I could not tell whether the smoke was from him or from the environment he had been in, it all still hurt. I thought that my lovingkindness would bring a breakthrough. It was exhausting. But my mind was set on loving him back to his "senses".

- *Be sensitive to the Holy Spirit. Ask Him to lead you and to teach you exactly how He wants you to demonstrate His love in every season.*
- *"Love without truth is not love and truth without love is not truth." – Lisa Bevere.*

Red Flag Alert: What I saw both scared and scarred me.

It took only but one conversation for me to snap. It was a conversation between my husband and a close friend of his. The conversation switched to the friend asking him if he was going to choose me, his wife or the girl he had been having an affair with for the past couple of months. He was unsure of his position; he then went on to compare the both of us and, in essence, weigh *the pros and cons.*

- *In God's mercy and loving kindness, He allowed me to see the true state of my husband's heart. When the Lord reveals things to you, He does so for a purpose. The question then becomes, what will you do with it?*

Red Flag Alert: One of the reasons I moved out, aside from the obvious with everything I saw on his phone, was that I no longer recognized myself. The words and language that had come out of my mouth, three weeks prior to the car chase incident, were foreign to even the unsaved version of me. Hearing them come out of my mouth signaled my need to create the necessary distance. In that state, with how troubled I was, I was not in the right frame of mind to continue praying for his restoration nor the restoration of our marriage.

- *When the enemy comes, he does not just come to steal, he also comes to kill and to destroy you and your relationship with Jesus. Never let him win by letting anger control you. For as James 1 says: "…the wrath of man does not produce the righteousness that God desires." (James 1:20 NKJV/NIV)*
- *What are some trials in your life that are pushing you to a point where you no longer recognize yourself?*
- *What is the Lord saying to you about how you are waging that war?*

Chapter 7

The Lord is My Helper

The day started off like every other Christmas day before it with lots of excitement at the thought of celebrating the birth of Jesus. I remember sitting in church worshiping and simply amazed at God's goodness and His grace. Right before the end of the service, my husband sent me a text asking if I wanted to come over to his parents' to have dinner with his family. I was surprised at the invitation because, although we had been communicating, however sparingly, we were not fully reconciled, nor had we celebrated anything together since the fallout started.

Red Flag Alert: Nevertheless, and against my better judgment, I accepted his invitation. I do not recall details about dinner other than it must have gone okay. Later that evening, we watched an NBA game together alone in the house basement. And, because of how passionate we both get when we watch a game, we must have teased each other about our support for the opposing teams. And in some ways, flirted with each other.

Somehow in the middle of that, we got a little cozy. We kept inching closer and closer together. The logical part of my brain told me to pull away. But, the emotional part of me thought "this man is my husband whom I have not been with in over eight months." That night, we slept together.

Was it good? *Yes.*

Did it change anything? *No.*

Matter of fact, it might have worsened our situation. Because, in some ways, I had convinced myself that being intimate with him would bring his heart back. It did not. Not in the true sense anyway. It made us civil, even friendly towards one another and gave us, or me rather, **a false glimmer of hope.**

We continued having conversations and even started talking about living together again. He told me he was done with the girl. And, of course, my broken heart believed him. But everyone else around me – my family, my friends, my pastors, my entire community – believed he was being disingenuous.

Red Flag Alert: Yet I held on to what I thought was real. I took a trip to Nigeria to spend the rest of the holidays with my family and to attend my brother's wedding.

And I agreed to live with him again after I got back from Nigeria.

During our conversations, we decided we would move into my parents' condo for some time since they were out of the country. *Up until that point, even after I moved out of the apartment we co-rented, I continued carrying the financial burden for everything, including the rent.* So, our plan was to terminate the lease and live at my parents' for a few months until we could get a place.

While I was in Nigeria, we spoke a lot. He said all the right things and we made plans to build our marriage again. In some ways, he sounded like the man I knew. There was still some discomfort in my mind, but I ignored it. I tried convincing everyone that he was back, but they did not buy it. At some point, I got into a fight with my family and everyone else because they could see that he was being manipulative, but I could not. I was completely trusting of him. They were very concerned for me, but I could not see it. Before I left Nigeria, it was decided that we would in fact not move into my parents' condo. We had already terminated the old lease, so we planned to stay at my parents' for a few days before moving to our new place.

Red Flag Alert: When I got back from Nigeria, he picked me up from the airport and we went to my parents'. Again, we slept together. And it felt like things were slowly getting back to our old norm. I was so wrong! Within a few days of being home, things began to unravel. One night, I asked if we could study "The Love Dare" 21-day devotional together, he refused. Later, I tried to get us to read the Bible and pray together, but he also refused.

In the middle of all this, more than once, I had noticed him being secretive with his phone the same way he had been since it all started. I expected things to stop as we worked on our marriage. Again, I was disappointedly wrong.

But I said nothing.

We were cleaning our old place in preparation for our move to the new apartment. While at it, I stopped by the apartment and went through lots of paperwork to get rid of old receipts and documents. I found two things that caught my eye. One, a receipt from a Motel stay. I looked at the date and it read May 30th, 2016. My heart sank. That was the night of our one-year anniversary. Only, I did not see my husband that night. Why? Because he supposedly had "schoolwork". Only for me to discover that on the night when he should have been home, he took the girl to a motel.

Why was I putting up with this?

Was I so emotionally bound to him I could not confront the truth?

Red Flag Alert: As I sobbed, I saw another document. This one was one of his bank statements. I looked through the transactions but could not believe what I saw. While I had been slaving to carry us financially, he had been sending money to the girl. Now, you must understand, at the time, I worked for the State Health Government and I was not making a lot of money. Yet, I continued paying our phone bills, his Car Note, and our rent.

He Was Supporting Another Woman and I Sent Him Packing

Everything else that was both of our responsibilities, I shouldered. Yet, here he was, sending money to his side piece. As I continued to look through, I saw another more recent bank statement which showed him sending a couple thousand dollars to the girl in the past week while we were at my parents' together.

I was livid.

In short, I confronted him about it and sent him packing. Afterwards, I blocked him on every block-able platform on my phone so he could not reach me. I then sent him an email letting him know the cost of everything I had paid for in the past year. Then I told him I was giving him until the end of the month to get his finances in order; that after that month, I would stop picking up his slack.

At that point, I made a decision that this man won't cause me to die of a heart attack or any other disease for that matter. Thereafter, I visited my Gynecologist (GYN) to get tested for Sexually Transmitted Diseases (STDs).

I remember walking into my GYN's office and stating the reason for my visit. The excruciating pain it took to explain to my GYN that my husband's infidelity and my persisting, naive love for him led me to being intimate with him without protection was indescribable. Over the course of the next two years, we were intimate ten or so more times. And, after every time, I would get tested.

So, over, and over I dealt with the shame of it. A big part of me felt that being intimate would prevent him from going back to the girl. It was a delusional assumption, a rounding error.

So, every time, I would get tested.

In the way only He does things, thankfully, the Lord caused my GYN to be very gracious. She provided a safe space for me to share, and she encouraged me even beyond her medical obligation. I firmly believe the Lord planted her there to be a source of comfort to me in a very difficult time. On more than one occasion, she would ask me how I was handling everything, if I was okay mentally and emotionally. And because I knew to expect those questions, I always tried to build myself up in the Lord's strength before going in there. And so, I would tell her that my faith, my family, and my community of believers were helping me get through. In essence, I saw it as an opportunity to tell her about Jesus and showcase His might.

**God is our Refuge and Strength!
He provides supportive people to help us
through trials.**

Over the next couple of weeks, I tried to get accustomed to my new norm. I continued to draw strength from the Lord and from the community He had graciously provided. I also continued the pre-bedtime routine of sitting before Him and having Him encourage my heart with His Word. As was to be expected, some days went great, and others were horrible. I spent a lot of time in His Word and in worship in song. Most times, I cried as I worshiped just because the pain was still there.

Nevertheless, I continued to rely on the Lord as my Help and my Shield. With time, I got stronger spiritually and emotionally. The Lord also helped me become comfortable with carrying my hair as it was. Partly because He somehow positioned seemingly random strangers to speak kind words to me about my hair. The compliments were endless and helped boost my confidence. I knew it was all God and I marveled that He bothered that much to encourage me in even those small ways.

I was in a good place because of the Lord and in spite of my lack of wisdom and discernment.

As I got stronger, I resumed praying for my husband to be restored first to Jesus and second to me. I met with my friends and community all the time. We got together to pray and intercede on behalf of my husband. On some nights, all I wanted to do was go off on him and, on other occasions, I let my tongue express words I would not dare repeat in front of Jesus… Nevertheless, my friends encouraged me to keep trusting the Lord. So, I did.

My husband was like a prodigal son. Until he came to his senses and returned to the Lord, our relationship could never work.

Soon after, still in the Spring of 2017, we tried counseling sessions with one of our pastors and his wife at our church. I enjoyed the sessions because I felt like we were addressing things that we needed to; it seemed like we were making progress. Nevertheless, after only a few sessions he 'fired' them and stopped attending. I wish I could remember what it was that triggered him, but it was so ridiculous and just one of his manipulative tactics that I guess my brain refused to store it.

Red Flag Alert: We seldom had conversations. And, when we did, they were tense because I had no doubt he was still with that girl; even with his repeated denials of the fact.

In the Summer of 2017, we tried counseling with another pastor and his wife at our church. Like before, the sessions seemed promising until he decided he no longer wanted to attend. Nevertheless, he and I were getting close again and had gone on a date or two during that time per suggestion from the pastor and his wife. Then, one day, after speaking with the pastor, we decided it would be a good idea for me to attempt to move back in with my husband. I did not know how my husband would react to it. But I reasoned that I had moved out when I was struggling with everything he was doing and therefore not in a position to really pray and since I was in a better place, I reasoned that it was a good move. So, on one September afternoon, because I had a copy of the house key, I packed up my things and moved into the apartment when he was not home. I reasoned that, "since we're going on dates and sleeping together and living apart, it only made sense to take that as the next step."

Ha-ha! I really did a lot of foolish things for that man. I laugh now at the memory of what happened when he came home but it was anything but funny.

When he came home, all hell broke loose. He said too many hurtful words, most of which I thankfully do not remember (only God could do that). But what I do remember him saying was:

Red Flag Alert: *"Chiso, you do not know me. I am not the same man you married. You see bottles of alcohol all over this house, I am telling you, I am not the same man. You knew me as (inserts the name I fondly called him) but I am not that person, I am (inserts his other name) now. You need to leave. If not, I will call the cops."* He also said something about wanting to finish his Pharmacy board exam first before moving in together. It all made no sense? Yes, I know.

Sigh.

"Umu nwanyi a tala afufu"

It is a saying in my language - the Igbo language. When translated to the English language it loses i*ts umph*. But in essence, it means that "a lot of women have suffered in life, particularly in the hands of men".

With tears streaming down my face, I packed my things and I left.

As that year came to an end, a few hours before January 1st, 2018, I made up my mind that I was no longer going to be his booty call. So, I sent him a message telling him that I was done with that role. I told him he should let me know when he was ready to be a husband and then I blocked his number.

For the first six months of 2018, we were not in touch. And then sometime in June, his mom had a thanksgiving service at church, and he showed up.

I remember for the duration of the service doing everything within my power to not look in his direction. It was hard, but somehow the Lord helped me. I was conscious of his presence there, but my resolve was strong to not give him even a momentary glance.

I attended the reception out of honor for his family and particularly, my mother-in-law. Sometime after the party, he reached out and we chatted a bit. I do not recall what we talked about. A few days later, he came over to mine. We watched a game together, chatted, and tried to catch up on each other's lives given it had been over 6 months of silence. It got late and I sent him back to his house. He came by a few other times over the span of the next few months and in some ways, it felt like we were rebuilding a friendship. I tried to keep him at arm's length. Sometimes I was successful, other times I was not. Things went on seemingly okay. Until the early hours of November 2nd, 2018.

It must have been sometime between midnight and 6:00 a.m., hard to tell the exact hour when I had the dream. Most of it was fuzzy. But what I do remember was that in the dream the Lord showed me two persons, one, a little boy and, two, *my husband as the boy's father.*

As I mentioned, I do not particularly consider myself a "Joseph". More often than not, I forget my dreams and only wake up when my alarm goes off. But, for whatever reason that night, the Lord decided to speak to me via a dream. To ensure I remembered it, when the day broke, I shared the dream with my friends and pastors. I moved on; dismissing the dream as a representation of a "spiritual baby" or "birth in the spiritual realm"; not an actual child.

A day or two later, I had one of my very dear pastor friends from Oklahoma over at mine for dinner. As we ate, I told her about the dream. She paused and then she said, "Chiso, usually when you see a baby in a dream, it does NOT typically mean a 'spiritual baby'. But let us pray and ask the Lord for clarity". And, yes, we prayed. Afterwards, I forgot all about it. My husband and I were in touch inconsistently but did not see each other for a few weeks.

As December 2018 got closer and, with it, the end of another year, I felt it impressed on my heart to seek the Lord in prayer with fasting. So, I set my heart to seek His face for 21 days. In times past, for as long as our marriage had been in turmoil, it always seemed that whenever I would set my heart to seek God with fasting and prayer, my husband would show up at my door. So, I had conversations with my friends to be on the alert with me and to keep me accountable.

And, just like clockwork, on night 1 of my fast, guess who showed up at my front door unannounced? My prodigal, manipulative husband. *Sigh.*

Red Flag Alert: His story? He had a long drive and was too tired to drive home so he asked if he could spend the night.

I know, dear reader, I can almost hear you screaming "NO" on my behalf…

I agreed on one condition, we would sleep on separate beds. I told him I was on a fast and did not want to be with him. He agreed to it. So, we laid on separate beds in the same room. We made pillow talk for a bit. As I drifted off to sleep, he called out to me and gave some phony story about wanting to come over to my bed to give me a massage.

Ugh.

I allowed it against my better judgment; being a sucker for those and, more than anything, I had missed his embrace all year long. Within minutes what started out as a massage quickly escalated to something more.

Afterwards as he slept soundly next to me, I crawled out of bed and went to the living room. I sat on the couch and cried silently so I would not wake the man snoring loudly in the next room; yes, the same man who had mastered the art of using me and hurting me over and over.

I texted my friends, my mentors, my pastor, and my pastor friend in Oklahoma to let them know what had happened. It must have been sometime after 1:00 a.m. I felt condemned. I felt like I could not figure out how to pull away from this man. I felt stuck. At that moment, I felt like I had let the Lord down. I just felt ashamed.

Then I got a message from my pastor friend in Oklahoma. She simply asked me if I thought the cross of Jesus was too weak to handle my decisions. She went on to remind me that there was no condemnation for me in the Lord and encouraged me with the Word of God. I know without a doubt that the Lord used her to minister to my heart that night. Eventually, I fell asleep on the couch. My husband came by and tried to get me to come back to the bed but I told him I was fine on the couch. And, right there in the early hours of that morning, I made up my mind that I would go for one last STD test and after that, I was really done with his yo-yoing.

I thought I had the strength and resolve with God's help to resist my husband's manipulations. Little did I know that I was on the brink of learning more things that would threaten to shake the foundation on which I stood.

The Lord is My Helper

Red Flag Alerts

As you continue this journey with me through my marital trials, pause and reflect on the Red Flag Alerts I failed to recognize or did not heed. Review this chapter and consider how you might have done things differently if you encountered a similar situation.

Red Flag Alert: Nevertheless, and against my better judgment, I accepted his invitation. Later that evening, we watched an NBA game together alone in the house basement. And in some ways, flirted with each other.

- *What should I have done differently in this situation?*

Red Flag Alert: Yet I held on to what I thought was real. And I agreed to live with him again after I got back from Nigeria.

- *What decisions are you making from an emotional standpoint?*
- *How can you switch that to allow the Lord to lead you to the truth?*
- *It is important to not be led by our emotions. The Bible teaches us the importance of being led by the Spirit and not by our flesh.*

Red Flag Alert: When I got back from Nigeria, we slept together. And it felt like things were slowly getting back to our old norm. I was so wrong! Within a few days of being home, things began to unravel. One night, I asked if we could study "The Love Dare" 21-day devotional together, he refused. Later, I tried to get us to read the Bible and pray together, but he also refused.

- *In what areas of your life do you feel that gentle nudge from the Lord letting you know something is off? Are you ignoring His nudge?*
- *Ask Him to expose the deception around you and to give you eyes to see.*
- *All that is hidden will eventually be exposed by the light.*
- *Now when I pray, I ask the Lord to show me any deception that I cannot perceive.*

Red Flag Alert: As I sobbed, I saw another document. This one was one of his bank statements. I looked through the transactions but could not believe what I saw. While I had been slaving to carry us financially, he had been sending money to the girl.

- *Is there someone you have been praying for the Lord to restore?*
- *In what ways are you unknowingly enabling their behaviors?*
- *What are some ways you can love them without enabling them?*
- *Ask the Lord how you can make some changes to continue to support and love them without enabling them.*

Red Flag Alert: We seldom had conversations. And, when we did, they were tense because I had no doubt he was still with that girl; even with his repeated denials of the fact.

- *Are there things in your life that the Holy Spirit is asking you to let go of?*
- *What are some ways you are justifying or trying to deny what you know to be true?*

Red Flag Alert: *"Chiso, you do not know me. I am not the same man you married. You see bottles of alcohol all over this house, I am telling you, I am not the same man. You knew me as (inserts the name I fondly called him) but I am not that person, I am (inserts his other name) now. You need to leave. If not, I will call the cops."*

- *As painful as this moment was, it taught me a valuable lesson: no amount of your power or your strength can restore the depths of spiritual brokenness in a person; only Jesus can do that.*

Red Flag Alert: His story? He had a long drive and was too tired to drive home so he asked if he could spend the night.

- *What temptations are you facing in your life right now?*
- *What are some ways the enemy is trying to convince you that you are strong enough to "go near" without falling?*
- *There is a reason the Word of God tells us "So, if you think you are standing firm, be careful that you don't fall" (1 Corinthians 10:12 NIV)*
- *Do not ever allow your desire to overrule the discernment the Lord has given you.*

Chapter 8

The Daniel Fast

It was January 15th, 2019, and I was on the phone with my best friend in England. We discussed the year ahead and our hopes for it. And, somewhere in the middle of that, we both *randomly* decided we would go on a fast together to start the year right.

> "...even the events that seem accidental are really ordered by Him." (Proverbs 16:33 AMPC)

We did not have anything that was on our hearts to seek the Lord about. We just felt like we wanted a "spiritual cleanse". I remember us joking about the kind of fast we would do. For as long as we have been saved, we always joked (and still do) that if the Lord were to give out medals for fasting when we get to Heaven, neither of us would be considered for even the most insignificant prize.

Finally, we decided on a "Daniel" fast for three days: the 16th, the 17th, and the 18th of January. We went back and forth trying to decide on the type of foods we would and would not eat. We even spent some time trying to figure out what was considered a vegetable/fruit and what was considered crossing the line. About the fast, the last conversation we had was about my husband's tendency to show up at my doorstep like he always did when I was on a fast. We came up with a plan to resist him through prayer.

On the first day of the fast, we barely made it through.

On the second day, we were on the brink of not surviving and had gone as far as modifying the "allowed" food items on our list. Honestly, I have never had a fasting and prayer exercise as "laid-back" as this one. It was a very "grace-laden" one, ha-ha.

That same evening, I got a call from my husband.

I ignored it. Then, I sent him a text:

Me: I can't talk right now. Text me?
Him: I was in the neighborhood so wanted to stop by to see what you were up to.
Me: I am at the gym and about to walk into a session with my personal trainer. Ttyl.

I informed my friend of what had happened. We made jest of it and continued our fast.
On the third day, we were happy to have *survived* the fast. We decided to break by 6:00 p.m. Due to the time difference between us (my friend being in the U.K., me in the U.S.), it meant that my friend would break 6 hours before I would. We agreed to break individually and pray together at a later time.

About three hours before 6:00 p.m., I was on the YouVersion Bible app and the Lord turned my attention to my display profile photo. The photo was of my husband and I. It was taken on the night of our wedding. It was the end of the wedding party, and we were both exhausted and walking out of the hall to head to our hotel room when someone stopped us for a photograph. With complete exhaustion, I stood behind him and wrapped my arms around his waist - more for support than anything. He stood in front and wrapped his arms around mine, with my makeup smeared all over the collar of his white shirt and his bow tie completely undone. Neither of us cared.

Our hearts were full and so we smiled for the camera. It was my favorite photo of us. For the past three years, amidst all the chaos, I left it as my profile photo on the Bible app as a sign of my faith and belief that the Lord would restore our marriage. As I sat in my chair at work, looking at the photo, I felt a sudden quickening in my spirit that it was time to take the photo down. It felt like it was the Lord, and I sensed His peace. Without wasting a thought on it, I took it down and replaced it with a photo of just me. Then, I sent a text to my best friend to let her know.

She was silent.

She replied saying, "I knew you were about to change it; the Lord told me. He has been sharing some things with me this afternoon. But, I am not released to say them yet." I was eager to hear what the Lord told her. However, knowing who she is and that she would not utter a word of it prematurely, I decided there was no point pressing her to divulge anything.

At 4:30 p.m., I packed up and left work to pick up one of my close male friends –my husband's accountability partner and one who had been by my side from the start of the turmoil, supporting and praying with me. It must have been a little after 5:00 p.m. when I arrived at his place. I sent him a text letting him know I had arrived. As I sat in my car waiting, I started counting the minutes until 6:00 p.m. and daydreaming about the Chick-fil-A meal I was going to devour then. I was lost in thought when a text came in at 5:12 p.m.; three back-to-back messages from an unknown number. The messages read, and I quote:

> "Your husband is paying my sister child support for their son."
> "If you don't believe me, look up his name on case search."
> "I'm telling you because I would want to know."

I read it again.

> "Your husband is paying my sister child support for their son."
> "If you don't believe me, look up his name on case search."
> "I'm telling you because I would want to know."

Red Flag Alert: And again. *"Your husband is paying my sister child support for their son. If you don't believe me, look up his name on case search. I'm telling you because I would want to know."*

In the blink of an eye, all the protective mechanisms in my body kicked in. It was as though there was a sudden shield that was thrown over my heart and my mind that prevented me from really comprehending what I had just read.

I forwarded the texts to the friend I was waiting on, my best friend in the U.K., two other friends here in the U.S., my pastor, and my pastor friend in Oklahoma. It was close to 6:00 p.m. and the only thing on my mind was Chick-fil-A and breaking my fast. I was too distracted to focus on anything else but food. After forwarding the texts, I put my phone on 'Do Not Disturb'. I barely remember what happened on the drive with my friend. He asked me some hard questions about the texts and the implications of it. I answered him without really knowing what I was saying.

On our way to my home where he would be borrowing my car for his use, we stopped by Chick-fil-A. After he left, my friends and my pastor called. I picked up the phone and spoke with them for a short while, but I have no recollection of the conversation. All I remember was them asking me if I was okay. My response was that I was and my suspicion was that one of my husband's girl toys was trolling me. I only dismissed the text thereafter.

I went into the house, put on one of the TV shows that always amuses me and laughed as I ate my Chick-fil-A. About fifteen minutes later, I was done eating, I turned off the TV and got ready for bed.

As I laid in bed, it took me a while to fall asleep but when I did, I had two dreams. I can't remember the details of the first one but, the second, I remember so vividly as though it happened only yesterday. In it, I saw my husband, a little boy, and a strange woman. Something was very strange about the scene. It looked like the woman did not want the child and my husband was left there with a boy. It is hard to describe what I saw. It seemed like I was looking at a very dysfunctional trio, but a trio, nonetheless. As soon as I saw the boy, I knew in my heart that that was indeed my husband's son.

I woke up shortly after with my pillow soaked and my face wet. I was so confused. I looked at the clock and just a few minutes had gone past 5:00 a.m. Apparently, I was crying in the dream and in real life simultaneously. And as soon as I realized the tears were from the dream, I knew.

I did not care what time it was. I got up, grabbed my toothbrush, and drove over to one of my friend's.

She came to the door and as I looked into her living room, I saw piles of used tissue scattered all over the floor. I looked at her and asked, "what is with all the tissues? Are you sick?"

Silence.

Red Flag Alert: I walked into her house, sat down, and told her I wanted to check the child services website to see if the text I received the previous night was true. I picked up my phone to pull up the website and she said, "No, use mine, I do not want the history and memory of it on your phone."

She pulled up the website, handed me her phone and sat in silence watching me as I looked at the result of my search.

I saw three names on the website:
1. My husband's name,
2. A woman's name, and
3. A third name.

The third name also happened to be one of my top three favorite biblical names and one I had written down on my phone as the name of the child I would someday birth for my husband. A strange woman had beat me to it.

Next to the third name was a birth date and somewhere on the page was the confirmation of my husband being the father of the boy and the court's ruling of the amount of money the judge was ordering my husband to pay in child support every month.

The last bit of information I gleaned showed the date of the ruling, January 17th, 2019. I thought for a second and realized the ruling had been confirmed on the second day of my fast. Going by the time stamp, I saw that shortly after the ruling was when my husband called me and later sent that text saying "...*I was in the neighborhood and wanted to stop by...*".

Silence.

I stared at the phone for a couple more minutes - which felt like an eternity - rereading and trying to comprehend it all. A few seconds later, I handed the phone back to my friend. I did not say a word.

I got up, grabbed my toothbrush, and went to her bathroom to brush my teeth. When I was done, I went back to the couch and sat in silence. I was strangely calm.

I picked up a Bible next to me and was led to this portion of Scripture:

> *"But now, thus says the Lord, Who created you, O Jacob, And He Who formed you, O Israel: 'Fear not, for I have redeemed you; I have called you by your name; You are Mine. When you pass through*

> *the waters, I will be with you; and through the rivers, they shall not overflow you. When you walk through the fire, you shall not be burned, nor shall the flame scorch you."*
> (Isaiah 43:1-2 NKJV)

And as my heart listened to Him comfort me, I let the silent tears flow; I saw no point in trying to stop them. My friend got up from the couch and held me and she and I cried together. Mine were silent tears, hers were more of a wail.

And then, I felt an overwhelming sense of peace; I felt a release in my spirit. I was free.

But I did not understand it.

My friend asked me what I was thinking/feeling, I told her I felt a release and said no more. I did not know what else to say, so I remained silent that morning.

At about 9:00 a.m., my friend's husband, being the church worship team leader, got ready to leave the house for practice, as it was typical of Saturday mornings. I am on the worship team as well and I decided to go for practice that morning, without breaking routine. As I sat in silence in my car waiting for him to pull out his car, the Lord began to speak to me.

Seemingly randomly, the Lord began to narrate a portion of Scripture to me, one with king David. It was 2 Samuel 12, where the prophet Nathan was sent by the Lord to rebuke David for his indiscretions. After that conversation, David took some time to seek the Lord and petition for mercy on behalf of his son. The Lord picked up the story in verse 16:

> "David begged God to spare the child. He went without food and lay all night on the bare ground. The elders of his household pleaded with him to get up and eat with them, but he refused. Then on the seventh day the child died. David's advisers were afraid to tell him. "He wouldn't listen to reason while the child was ill," they said. "What drastic thing will he do when we tell him the child is dead?" When David saw them whispering, he realized what had happened. "Is the child dead?" he asked. "Yes," they replied, "he is dead." Then David got up from the ground, washed himself, put on lotions, and changed his clothes. He went to the Tabernacle and worshiped the Lord. After that, he returned to the palace and was served food and ate. His advisers were amazed. "We don't understand you," they told him. "While the child was still living, you wept and refused to eat. But now that the child is dead, you have stopped your mourning and are eating again." David replied, "I fasted and wept while the child was alive, for I said, 'Perhaps the Lord will be gracious to me and let the child live.' But why should I fast when he is dead? Can I bring him back again? I will go to him one day, but he cannot return to me." Then David comforted Bathsheba, his wife, and slept with her. She became pregnant and gave birth to a son, and David named him Solomon. The Lord

> *loved the child and sent word through Nathan the prophet that they should name him Jedidiah (which means "beloved of the Lord"), as the Lord had commanded."* (2 Samuel 12:16-25 NLT)

I thought it was so random and I wondered why the Lord was telling me the story.

I got to church and all I did throughout worship practice was pour out my heart to the Lord. Every word of every song meant something. I was not just singing idly; my heart was hurting and so I expressed it in worship. Over and over when I could feel the tears building up and when no one was looking, I would sneak over to the bathroom. I would encourage my heart, wipe my tears, and go back out to practice. I was determined to not let anyone else know what was going on. I was determined to worship the Lord in song even through the tears. I did not actually tell Him what I felt, rather I sang to Him of His Love and His Majesty.

After practice, I went home to get some clothes for the weekend to stay at my friend's. I knew staying at home by myself would not be wise. When I got back to my friend's place, I remained quiet for the rest of the day. My mind was in a million places all at once. But, I did not actually speak with the Lord.

By evening time, there was an NBA game and, given my passion for all things basketball, I uttered my first words to the Lord:

Me: God, please let my team win.
God: Why won't you come to Me?
Me: Because I do not know what You are going to say.

God: Whatever I say, it will be for your good.

After that, I went to watch the game and acted like I did not know God was waiting on me. I sat and watched quietly as my team -LeBron James and the Los Angeles Lakers- got spanked by the Houston Rockets in overtime that night. The not-so-perfect ending to an already interesting day.

Shortly after, my friend's family gathered to pray. Without telling either of them anything, her husband had us turn to Psalm 27 and he read verses 1-14 out loud. When we got to verse 8, I paused as we read:

> *"My heart has heard You say, 'Come and talk with Me.'*
> *And my heart responds, 'Lord, I am coming.'"*
> **(Psalms 27:8 NLT)**

I stared at those words because I knew He was calling out to me. But still, I did not say a word to Him. I went to bed but kept tossing and turning until 4:27 a.m. when I decided there was no point struggling with God any further. I got up and decided to write. This was what I penned:

> *Jesus, You are...*
> *My Hiding Place,*
> *My Safe Refuge,*
> *My Strong Tower,*
> *My Place of Safety,*
> *My Glory,*
> *My Shield,*
> *The Lifter of my head,*
> *My Companion,*

My Sustainer,
My Ebenezer,
My Help,
The Rock on which I stand.

I read the verses in 2 Samuel 12:16-25. And then, I went to sleep.

The Daniel Fast
Red Flag Alerts

As you continue this journey with me through my marital trials, pause and reflect on the Red Flag Alerts I failed to recognize or did not heed. Review this chapter and consider how you might have done things differently if you encountered a similar situation.

Red Flag Alert: I walked into her house, sat down, and told her I wanted to check the child services website to see if the text I received the previous night was true. She pulled up the website, handed me her phone and sat in silence watching me as I looked at the result of my search.

I saw three names on the website:

1. My husband's name,
2. A woman's name, and
3. A third name.

The third name also happened to be one of my top three favorite biblical names and one I had written down on my phone as the name of the child I would someday birth for my husband. A strange woman had beat me to it.

- *What do you do when you get to that moment and you realize that all you have hoped and prayed for for the past three years is not going to come to pass?*
- *How do you respond?*

- *Do you blame God? Do you blame yourself? Do you blame satan?*
- *How should we respond in those moments?*

Chapter 9

God's Permissible Will

Daylight came quickly and, with it, the reminder to attend church that morning. I spent the entire weekend at my friend's place which meant I still had not communed with the Lord. I found reasons to avoid Him. Nonetheless, I made up my mind that as soon as the church service ended, I would go back to my house and sit before Him. At service, that morning, I worshiped the Lord and was present. I engaged with everyone as best I could, and I recall a conversation with one of the pastors who pulled me aside to ask for updates. I merely told him I was trusting the Lord and would know soon enough.

Afterwards, I drove home.

Of course, in the course of the three years I endured this turmoil, there were moments I got so upset with my husband that I declared "I was done." But, in my heart, I knew it was not that simple. I had surrendered my life to Jesus, therefore, any decision I had to make, especially as it pertained to the marriage covenant I was in, needed to include at least two of the three parties involved – Jesus, my husband, and I. As I had resolved to do, I sat before the Lord at 3:00 p.m. on Sunday, January 20th, 2019, to have the very painful but extremely necessary conversation.

It went thus:

Me: Papa, here's my question:
I feel released from my marriage to my husband. Is this Your permissible will?

God: "In the beginning, when you heard about all he had done, you immediately demanded a divorce. So, I said to you: 'I have not released you from this marriage'. I knew then that you had not even tried. You were just ready to quit.
But now, I have seen you.
I have seen you try and put in effort.
I have seen your labor.
And, I have matured you in this process.
That is why you sense that release now. Because the problem here is with a man's will."

Me: Please confirm it with Your Word

God: "I already did. I gave you the Word in 2 Samuel 12:16-25. As soon as you found out, I gave you that Word. When you could not sleep last night, yes, I spoke words of comfort to you, but I also gave you the answer you sought. You have sought Me. You have fasted and prayed and believed Me. But now, it is time to get up and turn the page. Where I am taking you will have this label 'Beloved of the Lord'. The glory of your latter shall be greater than your former."

I knew the journey ahead was far. And, as I sat there listening to the Lord yet thinking about the journey, fear started creeping in. But God sensed it and comforted me. He spoke these words to my heart:

> "*So do not fear, for I am with you; do not be dismayed, for I am your God. I will strengthen you and help you; I will uphold you with My righteous right hand.*" (Isaiah 41:10 NIV)

His words quelled my fears and I worshipped Him as I received His instruction. Next, I looked up some divorce lawyers. And, for the first time in the three years of my storm, the words on the screen were comprehensible. Then, I got up from His Presence, dressed up and was ready to drive to my pastor's house to inform him and his wife of my decision cum instruction from God. As I walked towards the door, I heard the bell ring. I went outside and alas!, it was my husband. I walked past him without uttering a word. I could not trust myself to not say something I would later regret. I went into my car and drove to my pastor's house. Later that day, I sent an email to my husband simply stating (paraphrase):

I am filing for a divorce.

I have decided to cite 'irreconcilable differences' so as to not bring shame to your name and taint your image but most importantly so as to not get your son dragged into this. However, if you decide to fight me on the divorce, or make it difficult in any way, I will, in no uncertain terms, explain to the judge everything that you have done over the past 3 years. I will tell all about your adultery and I will tell them all about your son.

My lawyer will get in touch with you.

Over the next couple of days, I began informing the people in my life. My parents were in Nigeria at the time and my five siblings were in different parts of the world. Hence, I had to break the news to them virtually. I convened a zoom meeting; first with my siblings and next with my parents. Tears welled up in my eyes, and even now, as I think back on that day, witnessing the joy my family expressed as they received the news.
My 12-year-old baby brother was in school at the time. He was very close to my husband, so I planned and told him in-person. I was nervous about his reaction, but he simply said: "God approves of it, and you are happy, so I am happy too."

Other pastors at our church were aptly informed as well. At this point, I had my resolve and was not seeking anyone's validation nor permission. My mind was made up. My goal was to inform those who had been by my side every step of the way. When I broke the news, one of the pastors was in awe and said to me:

'So, God loves you this much that He would go to the extent of allowing your husband to get a random woman pregnant just so He could reach you and convince you that it is time to walk away?! Wow.'

I met with and shared my story with a couple of lawyers. However, for a myriad of reasons, the cost of retaining one being a big one, I declined the offer to hire them. Little did I know that God already had it all figured out:

My father is a lawyer, my mother is a lawyer, and my baby sister is a lawyer.

At the time, my sister was working at a Law Firm in New York as a Corporate Lawyer. By some miracle, we were able to petition the court to have her represent me here in Maryland. Keep in mind, she was not practicing family law, nor did she have jurisdiction in Maryland. However, the Lord went before us and granted us favor. Furthermore, a dear friend and mentor of mine has a sister who is also a lawyer in Texas. So, together, my parents, my sister, and my friend's sister, i.e., my community of lawyers, lovingly walked me through the legal process.

My petition was filed on February 1st, 2019. I was scheduled to begin my Physician Associate (PA) program on May 23rd, 2019. So, amongst my many requests to the Lord, one other thing I asked was: *"Father, please let this divorce be final before PA school begins."* Furthermore, my sister (who was also my lawyer) was getting married in another country on April 20th, 2019, and I did not want it hanging over my head at the wedding. So, like Abraham in the Bible where he said:

> *"Now that I have been so bold as to speak to the Lord, though I am nothing but dust and ashes, what if…"* (Genesis 18:27-28A NIV)

I went to the Lord and asked Him to give me a date before April 20th so that I could fly out of the country for the wedding as a free woman, without my husband's last name. In His never-ending goodness and loving kindness towards me, He gave me a court date: April 12th, 2019.

There were some frustrations throughout the process. One in particular was when my husband sent a communication, via his lawyer, trying to secure any money he had recently come into. Mind you, I had played a significant role in financing this man throughout his time in Pharmacy school. So, I went crying to my sister (i.e., my lawyer) about the injustice of it all that I was beginning PA school with nothing. I had not asked for any of his money but that he would dare say that was hurtful. I felt like I had been working for years with nothing to show for it because I was busy covering my bills and his. But endowed with God-given wisdom, my sister said to me: "Let him keep his money. So that just like Abraham said:

> *"But Abram said to the king of Sodom, 'I have raised my hand in an oath to the Lord, God Most High, Creator of heaven and earth, that I will not take so much as a thread or sandal strap or anything else that belongs to you, so you can never say, 'I am the one who made Abram rich.'"*
> (Genesis 14:22-23 CSB and NLT)

…he will also never be able to say, "I made Chiso rich." Do not worry, God will take care of you, and He will bring your own."

Given these reasons, I let my husband know that I wanted no part of anything he owned. In addition, I told him I wanted no part of anything else I left in the house. I was walking away from it all with my name and whatever was left of my dignity.

April came and with it varying emotions. On one such night, I penned the following:

The Process of My Release…

> *"God, You're such a safe and powerful place to find refuge! You're a proven help in time of trouble—more than enough and always available whenever I need You. So, we will never fear even if every structure of support were to crumble away. We will not fear even when the earth quakes and shakes, moving mountains and casting them into the sea. For the raging roar of stormy winds and crashing waves cannot erode our faith in You. Pause in His presence"* (Psalms 46:1-3 TPT)

I certainly did not expect it to hurt as much as it did. On the one hand, I was beside myself with excitement when the Lord released me. I had fought for so long, and to finally have the burden lifted, I felt God's peace. Yet, the separating of two lives that had been joined in holy matrimony for four years and, before that, woven together in friendship for over six years (ten years in total) hurts a lot.

I have heard it said that until you have walked a mile in someone's shoes, you are unable to tell what they feel. Yet, I dare say, walking a mile does not give you a true glimpse of someone else's pain.

I keep hearing the Lord speak to my spirit:

"…I am the lifter of your head."

I am hearing it repeatedly. I am trying to pray but I cannot shake it. It sounds so loud in my heart, almost like someone has a loudspeaker next to me and is yelling it.

So, I continue the journey. I am in the throes of the divorce process. I am ten days from my divorce being final on April 12th, 2019. And I cling desperately to the Lord.

He is indeed the lifter of my head.

He has given me a gem in "Divorce Care", a support group designed to help people walk through their season of divorce and guide them with Biblical principles. Weirdly enough, I consider them my Tuesday night family. The leaders have been nothing but an absolute Godsend to me. It is a joy to learn from and be strengthened by others in the group who are walking the same path. I am eternally grateful to Jesus for this community. He truly is our Shepherd Who supplies us with all we need.

While I know not what awaits me, this I know, Jesus Christ is faithful. He has been with me, and He will not leave me now. As I move on in life, I remember the man I married. When I do, as the Lord leads me, I fall on my knees, and I ask the Lord to have mercy on him and to restore him back to Jesus. I ask the Lord to open his eyes and deliver him. Next, I pray for his son, and I ask that he be a good father to the boy and that the boy would grow up knowing that he is dearly loved. Finally, I pray that the boy would not have to suffer for the mistake of his parents.

Then, I move on to myself, I ask the Lord to search my heart and give me the grace to constantly forgive my husband.

I receive from God the grace to love him as Christ commands, not as my husband, but as someone whom God loves.

Finally, I receive the grace to not harbor bitterness in my heart towards him. In myself, this is impossible. But, not with God. With God all things are possible.

So, in God's strength, I release the man I married from my heart, and I walk away from him and into all that the Lord has for me.

April 12th, 2019 came and with it, the finality of my divorce and my marriage.

Sometime in August 2019, months after the divorce, I had an honest conversation with the Lord, and I said:

"Lord, I know that You are able to restore a marriage even after a divorce. But, after much pondering in my heart, I have concluded that I want nothing more to do with my ex-husband. I wish him well, but I do not want him. So, even though I know You can restore him in his relationship with You - and I pray You do, as I would never wish hell on him - give him another wife. Not me. I am done with that man."

A Final Word about THE Man in My Life

My heart is saturated with Joy because of The Calm in My Storm, JESUS. I remember sometime during the waiting period, not knowing what would happen yet trusting the Lord, I had been praying earnestly for the restoration of my marriage. During that period, I got close to a colleague, and it had been on my heart to share about God's goodness. But, at the same time, I would say to myself, 'No, Chiso, wait. When God restores your marriage, the testimony will be even more impactful.' On one such day while encouraging her about something else, the thought came back to share my testimony. Again, I said to myself, 'No Chiso, wait'. In that moment, I heard the Lord say to me: "I know you have been asking Me for restoration in your marriage. But what I want you to realize is that I have done an even greater restoration: I restored you in your relationship with Me. And that in of itself is the number one testimony of this season and impactful enough to share with the world."

Right then it hit me, I had been so blinded by my desire, albeit a noble desire, for my husband to come home that I missed the fact that my greatest testimony was in the restoration of my relationship with Jesus and how through what the enemy meant for evil, God turned it around and through it made me fall more in love with Jesus than ever before.

So, as you walk through your storm, my earnest prayer is that you will know with a deep sense of knowing that:

1. *You are not alone. Jesus Christ is right there with you, holding you close.*
2. *God will bring beauty from all your ashes. I was broken beyond repair, and He has, and still is, putting me back together even better than before. If He did it for me, surely, He can and will do it for you, too.*
3. *God remains blameless.*

Dear Heavenly Father, I pray for my brother or sister holding this book in their hands. Jesus, Your understanding of their pain, no one can fathom. I know You are intimately aware of them, and You love them dearly. I pray Sweet Holy Spirit, that You wrap Your arms around them and comfort them. You Who gathers all their tears, I pray that as You did for me, You wipe the tears from their eyes and give them joy for their mourning and show them that You are in absolute control of their lives and will bring purpose from their brokenness in Jesus Name, I pray. Amen!

**I love you with all my heart
and with the love of Jesus Christ.**

Epilogue

The Lord is Always with You

I wish I could promise you that you would walk away from your trial and be instantly healed, but the converse is true. Healing is a process, and you will invariably experience some triggers on your way to feeling whole. What I can promise you, however, is that through that, you will experience God's faithfulness and companionship in a way that is real and more tangible than the very air you breathe.

About a year after my divorce, I went through Christian counseling/therapy. Of course, I would have no other counsel outside of the Word of God. So, the Lord, in His goodness, sent a Pastor who is also a certified Christian counselor and Therapist to me. She was the icing on the cake as far as God's blessings go. Throughout my therapy process, I had some difficult healing periods. One of which I wrote about in my journal. At the risk of exposing my heart and being vulnerable, I will only share an excerpt:

> "For My thoughts are not your thoughts, and your ways are not My ways." This is the Lord's declaration. "For as heaven is higher than earth, so My ways are higher than your ways, and My thoughts than your thoughts…" (Isaiah 55:8-9 CSB)

Even as I read, I feel tears streaming down my face. I know His Word is true. I know His Word does not lie. But, this hurts. This was not what I envisioned when I said "yes" to him. I can almost hear him recite his vows. I remember the confidence and sincerity in his voice that made me feel secure. We could not contain our joy. Finally, we were husband and wife. Nothing and no one could take that away from us. I remember it all like it happened yesterday.

Yet, here I sit, months removed from the divorce with an aching heart.

"The task for therapy this week is something called 'exposure therapy'", she echoed. As those words fell on my ears, my heart sank in response. I thought to myself "you want me to do what?!" And then, a gulp - a silent one. In essence, the task was to go through one of his social media accounts and expose myself to see him. The objective was to build the capacity to stand my ground, not be moved, so that if I happen to run into him or come face-to-face with him at an unexpected place or time; I would have been exposed to him. I admire God's grace upon my therapist's life. Also, I know He has graced her with wisdom to counsel, therefore, I heeded her words, shuddering on the inside yet knowing there is wisdom in it.

So, I searched for him on the internet.

Then, I immediately sent a text to my therapist:

Me: *This exposure therapy is a little hard with seeing my ex :(*

Therapist: *What do you feel?*

Me: I feel a little crummy... I know God's ways aren't my ways, but it just feels like my ex got a pass.

Therapist: It appears as if he got away with mistreating you, but God's Word is sure. What a man sows that shall he also reap. And evil doers will soon be cut down. God doesn't always provide punishment right after an offense. But God's Word does not fail. He will reap it. God wants you to trust His total process through healing and forgiveness.

Me: Okay. Honestly it is a little hard for me right now... But I will try to put God's Word at the forefront to help me think differently.

Therapist: Jesus replied: "You don't understand now what I am doing, but someday you will." (John 13:7 NLT)

There it was. She spoke the truth, God's truth. And, through it, reminded me where to fix my gaze. So, I took that, and I ran with it. I sat before the Lord, and I opened His Word. And, even as I read, I cried. I read some more, and I cried a little more. Until He showed me this:

> "You will indeed go out with joy and be peacefully guided; the mountains and the hills will break into singing before you, and all the trees of the field will clap their hands." (Isaiah 55:12 CSB)

He said in a certain place:

> "...*Let God be true, and every human being a liar.*"
> (Romans 3:4 NIV)

In another place:

> "*Every Word of God is pure, He is a shield to those who take refuge in Him.*" (Proverbs 30:5 CSB)

And finally,

> "*Friends, do not avenge yourselves; instead, leave room for God's wrath, because it is written, Vengeance belongs to Me; I will repay, says the Lord. But if your enemy is hungry, feed him. If he is thirsty, give him something to drink. For in so doing, you will be heaping fiery coals on his head.*" (Romans 12:19-20 CSB)

To the natural mind, His is an "upside down" Kingdom. But, truly, it is the right way up. So, the way we expect things to happen - the natural order of things on this earth - differs from how He operates. Nevertheless, this I know, His way is better. So, dear child, you can rest in this.

Three Days Later, I wrote in my journal...

Looking back on that night, I recall that as my heart pondered those matters, I heard the Holy Spirit say to me "What would you give in exchange for My peace?" To be completely honest, I pretended not to hear Him. I was too upset.

The morning after the "exposure therapy", I had a session with my therapist, and I expressed exactly how I felt. And, as we conversed, the Lord used her to remind me of His goodness and His Word over my life. She spoke His truth over me and reminded me who I am in Jesus. It was refreshing listening to it, and I could sense faith rising on the inside. It reminded me of the Scripture that says:

> *"Two are better than one because they have a good return for their labor: if either of them falls down, one can help the other up. But pity anyone who falls and has no one to help them up."*
> (Ecclesiastes 4:9-10 NIV)

I was "down", and she used the powerful Word of God to pick me up.

That morning, I sat before the Lord, and He began to speak through the book of Nahum. Remember when Jonah went to speak to the people of Nineveh and he gave them the Lord's warning, and they repented? Well, fast forward 100 years later, they had gone back to their wickedness. So, the Lord sent another prophet, Nahum, to comfort His people and pronounce judgment on the nation. When I read this in my Bible, immediately, the Holy Spirit began to whisper to my heart that He is a just God. He reminded me that it is impossible for me to be more just than He is. He reminded me that everything He does is right. When He pardons, He is in the right, when He brings wrath, He is also in the right. He reigns supreme and He has, and always will have, the monopoly on wisdom.

I believe that the Lord is pouring out in my heart the revelation of His love and His goodness. His faithfulness respects no hurt we have experienced. Hence, on the mountains and in the valleys, His faithfulness stands.

In the Bible, we find that when the Lord alludes to avenging a person or a nation, oftentimes, the person does not live to witness the wrong avenged. Because, the way we want God to answer and pay back for the way we have been wronged is not necessarily the way He wants to do it. We must remember that, in everything God does, He does it to the glory of His name. All His actions magnify His name. It is always about Him. It will always be about Him. So, during the hurt and in the midst of walking through healing, our heart-cry should be: "Father, perfect all things for Your glory".

As I write these words today, I have forgiven my ex-husband and I trust that the Lord will reward him in a way that only He knows. Nonetheless, I shall admit that this forgiveness was a process. For a long time, after the divorce, a random memory would come to mind and when it did, I would find myself literally opening my palms to Heaven and symbolically releasing the hurt to the Lord, like an offering. For a while, I had to do it repeatedly until I no longer needed to do it.

So, as you walk through your process, I want you to know that our God is faithful, He will help you as He helped me. At first, the pain will be excruciating, but with time, He will heal and increase your capacity to keep on moving. He will do this simply because His plans are for your good and for your peace; the peace that is not moved by the presence of your storm.

Jesus is our example. Even as they mocked Him and did everything wrong to Him on the cross, He loved them with an everlasting love. This love drove Him to the cross. We are called to do the same; to love the very ones that hurt us. For Scripture reminds us that loving everyone that loves us is next to nothing. But, choosing to love the unlovable or those who have caused you the greatest hurt? Now in that, Jesus is glorified.

Receive the Grace of our Lord Jesus Christ, the Love of God, and the Sweet Fellowship of the Holy Spirit. May it rest upon you and teach you to forgive anyone who has hurt you and help you to walk away unmoved by their actions.

May the Lord bless you, in Jesus' name, Amen.
- Chiso Ori Uko

About the Author

Born and raised in Nigeria, along with her parents and 5 siblings, Chiso Ori Uko moved to the United States in 2006, at the age of 17, for college. Her four loves are Jesus, her family and friends, and her patients. Chiso has a heart for Worship, is an avid reader, a fitness enthusiast, and enjoys swimming and all things professional basketball. Fluent in her native language Igbo, she is now learning Spanish as well as working on perfecting her guitar and piano playing skills.

She is a Physician Associate who resides in Columbia Maryland, USA.

You can connect with Chiso on Social Media Instagram: @Chisoori or via Email at Thecalminmystorm@gmail.com

Milton Keynes UK
Ingram Content Group UK Ltd.
UKHW020826050923
428087UK00016B/1150